1

CONTENTS

2

CONTENTS (CONTINUED)

ACKNOWLEDGEMENTS

The real victims of the atrocities of slavery and racism in America are the millions of Africans who were brought to America against their will, made slaves, punished and killed, raped, farmed like animals and later emancipated into a racist society. I sincerely hope, as they lived and died, their souls were taken to a better place where living free and joyful is the standard.

Present day Black Americans still endure racism on a major scale in every aspect of their lives as well. I want them to know, I am fighting for you, I am praying for you and I will ensure action is taken towards the equality black people so much deserve from America.

To my Mother, Father and Brother Cary, the only reason I am the man I am today and a positive and caring person is all due to you. God has led me through you to be brave and fight against racism for the world. Thank you and I love you all!

My wife Shina is the greatest support of my dream and I could not have done this without her great support and encouragement. I love you and continue to learn something every day from you.

WHAT DO WE HAVE TO DO!

What do I have to do for the outright and equal standing cherished and deserved by every individual human being on earth? Is it me or do I feel unwelcomed and unwanted in a split societal chaos black people many years ago, helped develop and flourish? I have been the unending entity you used to build your riches and entertainment while sitting on the porch with a whip in one hand and a gun in the other. I have been the strong but broken person who gave you the reason to fight a brother against brother war resulting in little more than a transformation of slavery to pure racism and hate. I unknowingly gave you the ability to unify and hate me equally while telling me, "All men are created equal." I still question that statement and what it means to the United States of America. Why am I looked upon today and still feel there is a major problem with you? I would like to walk into a store dressed appropriately and not be prosecuted for shoplifting while another Caucasian man is shoplifting. I was told by my elders to look to the future and forget about the past, it is not in my heart to be able to do something so profound and irresponsible. I have never requested anything from you but the ability to live my life without shame and to see my children grow up in a now failing society that willingly accepts and will nurture their abilities. So why must I have to point out the obvious black elephant in the room of decency in our unfortunate society?

I am just a normal and caring man who is trying to make a good life in a disturbing country that I was introduced in an unfortunate way. How could any decent and educated living person feel it was right and just to take freedom away from one group of people to maintain freedom for another group of people? Without hate in my heart and deliberate violence pouring from my veins, I am trying to understand why this happened to our race? I am trying to understand when and how you thought it was a good thing to destroy the lives of millions of people for your economic advancement. Regardless of why this unfortunate circumstance happened, I would like to know when it is truly going to be over. If you feel history has shown a few instances of freedom for myself and other non-white people, think again and really look at the treatment of non-white people today. Choose any ten-magnificent people of color you see walking down the street and ask them directly about the treatment of their wellbeing and the confidence they have in being in this so called free country daily. I can admit, the freedoms in the United States are unmatched compared to other countries but the actual thoughts in people's minds about me do not make the "nice factor" but the "I cannot believe we are still here factor." It does not matter how educated, wealthy, prominent or heroic we may become many racist and uneducated people in this unfortunate country still look at us with content in their eyes and hatred in their heart.

Have black people in this derogatory country become so "white washed" they have forgotten how to live culturally in an outlandish country that clearly does not want them around? As mentioned previously, when I walk into a store, I am repeatedly asked, do I need any help? The translation for asking me for help is please, do not steal anything and I am going to watch you very closely because you are black and of course black people are the only race of people who steal. Apparently, every black person is a thief and a criminal regardless of their status or education level. I am sure many white people want us to either leave this country, "our country" or go back to suppressed status. Of course, they will never admit it because that would make them want what most racist white people are thinking. How do we keep black people inferior to white people even though I thought we were all on the same team and in the same free country? Unless you have been underneath a rock for most of your life, it is not hard to watch television and understand who tries in every way to be the most dominant and persuasive people. If you are asking for an example of this racist and opinion aided culture on television, you do not have to go any further than "FOX News." However, there are many more examples of racism on public and private television.

When I was in elementary school around 3rd grade, I was sitting in class and the very limited and educated teacher started talking about American history. She started talking about how all black people (not a true statement) were slaves and treated poorly throughout their entire lives during the time of slavery. I went to a mostly if not 95% white school so of course the white children all looked back at me with a look of strangeness in their eyes. That is the first day I believe most of the white kids in my class began thinking they were first class citizens and I was second class. This was the first day I realized I was truly different and I was not going to have it as easy as I once might have thought. Also, that very same day, I could tell who had racist parents and who did not by the amount of so called friends I lost in one week, and the new friends I gained immediately. Can you imagine, sitting in class and not knowing one day you would be embarrassed in a historical way without any warning? I felt the entire world change dramatically that day and I have been fighting the entire world ever since. I will mention how sports and physical activities bound a group of us together for life and we were all different races.

When is the last time you sat down at the park and watched kids play together? Do you notice how innocent and how unobstructed they play with each other? Children do not see color, they do not see gender, they see an opportunity to get to know another person and play any kind of game if it is fun. Can you imagine if we as grownups, who have already been affected with knowledge and society, took it upon ourselves to live in the same manner as innocent children only when it comes to accomplishing our mission of living our lives to the highest possible standards? It would be wonderful to love and let live and only see another amazing person trying to learn something about each other without a cloud of hate and society blocking your view. Children are innocent and without the opinions of callous people with hate in their cold and black hearts. One day I truly believe you will understand how bad things have become in this world and society due to the unfortunate beginning and history of black people in America.

What did you think was going to happen when television movies such as "Roots" and various shows depicting slavery hit the airwaves? It is interesting to think how society felt "Black Gangster Movies" invoked violence on a National level when it actually did not. Indiscriminate television movies depicting slavery created more violence and changed people's views about everything they once thought they knew about Black History. Of course, school at every level only introduced us to slavery and the mistreatment of black people. This history lesson did not include the horrible things these television movies showed such as the name calling, lynching, rape, true inequality even after slavery ended or the struggle of slaves who did everything in their power to ensure the escape of many slaves to the North, considered the free-states at that time. As I remember, the day after "Roots" was aired initially I personally wanted to lash out at every white person I saw, regardless of age or gender. I only wanted to inflict the incredible pain I saw on television of slaves onto white people and see how fast they would give up life. I was never a slave, I have encountered a lot of racism in my time but I was never a slave so I could not begin to imagine the true feelings or hardships they, as slaves went through. I can only speak for the actual racism I have encountered personally, however as bad as racism feels in my heart, without the physical part slaves encountered, slavery had to be defined as a living hell on earth.

Can I tell you the dream I had about three years ago when I was in another country defending this great nation of ours? I wanted to find the worst slave plantation ever created and ran by terrible white slave masters with an iron fist. A deadening place where slaves were repeatedly mistreated, women raped and children were born into slavery and died of old age with shackles still on their feet, knowing only slavery. Definition of cruelty and brutality, slaves being killed for even thinking about running away and feet being cut off for even less. Trees full of hanging dead slaves and tree trunks scattered with slaves who were tied up so tight their organs and fluids leaked out of their bodies slowly and painfully. Every baby born to slave women were all products of the rapes encountered nine months prior by perverted slave masters. Slaves were beat for not producing enough cotton to sell and make the high profits at market. Food given to slaves was the lowest quality and usually made them sick and unable to work where once again they would get beat until death or until they tried to work almost dead on their feet (literally). After seeing how horrible this plantation portrayed slavery, this is what I wanted to do. I wanted to switch the souls of every slave with every plantation owner and channel the feelings of every person into a journal and read it to the entire institution of slavery. I want the founding

forefathers to feel first hand slavery and how souls were destroyed and lives were

taken for the benefit of another people. Sometimes the only way to make people

understand pain is to let them feel it for themselves. My dream would be the

ultimate in learning from your mistakes through harsh example and reality. I still

do not understand how any race of people could effectively and routinely use

another race of people for economic benefit while mistreating and disregarding

their freedom?

NEGATIVE TRANSFORMATION

When African people were brought to America and used as slaves because white people at that time were too damn lazy to work for themselves, negative outlook on these African slaves was called racism. Is there another popular word for how black people were treated, degraded and otherwise discarded like trash thrown into the streets? During this incredibly horrible time of slavery, when a black person was seen regardless of his/her level of education or freedom, a white person would think of them as a slave and of the lowest quality disgusting person that ever lived. I cannot imagine how it must have been to be a part of that timeframe and endure the atrocities African slaves had to endure at the cold hands of greedy and disgusting slave owners. Every person who was not provocatively white was wrong in the eyes of every single white person who lived during this timeframe. I cannot put my finger on the thought processes of racist and horrible white people during this unfortunate period coming from anywhere but the dominant evil present in the human soul. Personally, I could not have stood by and watched other people of a different race work for me and not get paid and be forced to do so with harsh punishment and horrible treatment. Furthermore, rape, kill and torture these same people when they try to revolt and be treated equally and fairly. I just cannot see myself able to make that happen and not have a single regret in the world. Well, as we all know, once slavery was so called abolished, do you think the act of racism was over in America?

I am not trying to provide a history lesson on slavery but I am going to tell you how feelings from that era have changed into present day racism. We all know it was not a very popular decision to abolish slavery and let these black people live free in a society that once regarding them as second to fifth class citizens. I believe a new comedy act which included "Blackface" was created showing the newly released slave as an ignorant person who could not possibly make it in white society. Do you think white people would give the newly released black people a chance to live freely in their society? The answer to this question was not, in a major way. Black folks were still a commodity to white folks and were used as such even though they were to be paid and treated respectfully. Do you think a black person shortly after being released from slavery was treated fair and paid anything close to the white person doing the same job? No, white people still looked at black people as loose monkeys from the wilderness. Monkeys who white people were never going to let prosper in white society as an equal or even below that standard.

Free black people were still being killed and tortured at an alarming rate during this time of freedom and prosperity. It was very legal to kill, rape and destroy black people in the eyes of white America. It was also illegal for black people to be seen with white people or commit any crime of any kind without death by hanging as the outcome of an unfair legal trail. Black people had no freedoms, they had no happiness, and they were being mistreated due to the choice and abolishment of the horrible institution of slavery. It is hard to imagine how racist and uneducated white people were so upset about something their government decided to institute and even worse than that, to imagine how white people thought it was a bad decision to have decency and concern for a fellow human being. Black and white people bleed the same blood, have feelings, grow old in the same manner as each other and most definitely are both humans, most of the time. I personally think arrogant, egocentric and brutal white people of the past were not human at all, but the Devil who manifested itself up to power with death and destruction as its keys to success. Futile dominance through death and destruction is nothing but the omission of knowledge and the absence of kindness. I just want to know exactly what was going through hate filled white people's heads during slavery and after it was abolished. By the way, white people claimed they had and were following religion with slavery. I cannot imagine what kind of religion allowed the atrocities of slavery but if they say they possessed religion, I do not want any part of that religion.

Officially, the end of slavery was in the year 1865 but the final year of racism has not come and I imagine it never will. If there are ignorant white people in this world, racism will always be present. I have heard crazy words such as: "The South will raise again" and "Go back to Africa" for several years of my lifetime and I wonder what percentage of racist and ignorant white people in

America really agree with these hateful words? White people brought black people and other people to North America to do the work they were too damn lazy to do, treated them like dirt in every way, fought wars and spilled blood on both sides, black people built your country on their backs, reproduced by the millions and after all of this "history" you think it will be easy for all black people, mixed and pure, to "Go back to Africa." Black people might feel a little unappreciated with such ignorant words coming out of racist and stupid white people's mouths. Moreover, where in the hell do you think we could go in Africa where we would be accepted peacefully? We are not the same original people who were taken/given away/forced to come to America in the 1600-1800s. Our culture has been changed, our look has been changed and everything about Africa that was inside of our hearts has long been wiped away and forgotten. The only thing I know about Africa, and I am sure I am speaking for a lot of black people are what I read in books and seen on television.

I want to skip all the way up to what is considered present day when it comes to the treatment of black people in America. Oh, I know we are considered free and can do as we please in this great nation of ours but in the eyes of most black people, this freedom still comes with a price. I am not going to discuss how racist Television has become or how simple mistreatment of black people still goes on today until later but I want to portray specific events of one day. Just one day!!! To do this, I am going to begin in the morning at 7 am and end at night in the 11 pm timeframe.

MY BLACK PERCEPTION

Imagine if you will what you go through on any given day in the United States regardless of your color, race, creed, religion or gender and multiply that unnerving feeling by 100 and you have the average day for a black man. I live in a city I will not name and on a street named after a famous person from long ago. I wake up around five in the morning so I can get ready to drive 10 miles to my job which I have been doing for around 18 honest years. While I am walking to my awesome car in the parking lot, it is still kind of dark outside and I see an unattractive white lady walking to her used car also to go to work and a strange and familiar look comes upon her ugly face. We are the only two people in the parking lot and I can tell she now has a different attitude only verified when she rushes into her car and locks the doors immediately. Remember, I have been in this nice and expensive apartment complex for over three years and I have seen this particularly unattractive lady more than 20 times in the parking lot. If I was not so used to being treated this way, my eventful day would already be ruined. Interesting enough, I saw the same ugly lady that same afternoon and because other white and Hispanic people were in the parking lot with us, she even had the audacity to say hello. Only in America can this happen on a regular basis and it not be strange.

Now I am going to drive to work with a lot of other cars on a congested road and I have only enough gas to reach the gas station on the same road I have lived on for over three years. Of course, like every other car on the road, my registration and insurance are paid and I drive maybe a little over the speed limit on occasion. But unlike other drivers, I have a very nice vehicle and some police men do not think it is right for me to own such a nice vehicle and do something we in the black community call "Racial Profiling" to try and find something wrong with me. So, I am in a group of vehicles all driving the same speed and suddenly out of the blue, I get pulled over for no apparent reason and told to step out of my expensive and very clean vehicle. Since I know I have no chance at proper and equal treatment, I refuse to step out of my car because I know that is a good way to get myself into real trouble with backward ass country fuck police men who want to eagerly throw me in jail. I ask, "What is the problem" and the police man decided to want to know, where I was going and tell me nothing about why I was being stopped. Well after checking my license and registration and finding nothing wrong, he decided to want to do a search of my vehicle, let me remind you that I still do not know why I have been pulled over at this point. I refuse this as well and now another police car has pulled up and two more police men get out of this car to cover me. I still refuse to do anything the police men have ask so after another 15 minutes of checks and calls to their police station, I am released without ever knowing why I was pulled over in the first place. Only in America can this happen on a regular basis and it be considered an acceptable practice.

Now I need to stop and fill my car up with gas at the same gas station I have been going to ever since I moved to this city and state. I must go to this same gas station once a week at least and the same couple of people provide service. Interesting thing is when I go into the store to buy a drink or something with 10 other people in the store, I am the only person who is watched from the time I walk into the store until I leave. When I finally get to the front of the line I always ask the ignorant and obviously racist cashier why he always watches me when I see other people, white people putting things into their pockets without paying. The cashier never has an answer and I do not understand why I continue to go to this racist gas station except for the fact I know it will probably be the same situation wherever I go. I am dressed better than all of the other people, clean, smell good with cologne, speak proper English but because I am a six-foot three and 250-pound black man I am treated like I am a criminal and already convicted in the eyes of racist white Americans. Once again, only in America can this sort of treatment be the norm.

After filling my vehicle up with gasoline and buying a couple of drinks for the beginning of my day, I now must drive the remaining miles to my job. I am in America and I am black so this drive is going to be filled with police men turning their heads looking for the opportunity to give me a ticket regardless of what I am doing on the roads. Maybe they will find an unregistered hand gun or a good amount of drug I must be transporting to sell later. Either way, any ride for me on any street is filled with uncertainty and racism. Some may feel I am overreacting or going too far but nevertheless, I already know the average day of racism that America provides for any person who is not blond haired and blue eyed. Sometimes I feel like I am in the early 1900s and the events frequently happening is considered "acceptable" for the time. I finally get to work without any more incidents and begin my day.

My job is interesting and something I have been doing for a long time but seem to surprise people when I tell them what I do. I am a computer technician/programmer who loves what he does and is very good at producing results. First, remember I am a six foot, three and 250-pound black man and those two things do not go together for a few reasons. People who work in the computer sciences are considered intelligent and geeky. When people see who I am and realize I am there to help them with their computer technology I seem to get the wondering mind's eye. You can tell me all day and night they act like this because I am the athletic type and not the computer geek type, but the real reason comes from me being the black type and not the white type. Once again, do you think I am paranoid to be this way, even though I have been on this earth for over 40 years? I am confused about one thing, who proved that black people are not intelligent? Besides the racist white pigs who forced black people to become slaves and did everything in their power to keep a lid on our ideas and independence.

Why do racist and ignorant white people think it is acceptable to treat intelligent and proud black people as second-class citizens in this day and time? I do not feel I need to look over my shoulder every day or wonder when I am going to be a victim of American racism. It is not fair and I will not let it go on any longer. I have risk my life for this country and loved every minute of it because I still believe in the freedom I was promised way back in the late 1800s. Racism is in every aspect of my life but things are going to change one way or another.

FAILURE

Music is dynamic and diverse in general and pertains directly to racism in America and all over the world for that matter. Music has been a way of expressing our views of the world in our own piece of life to the public eye. There is one type of music that started in New York in the park to have fun and talk about the events of the day and the way you felt life was going in your own neighborhood. Funny thing about this expression of music originating way back in ancient times is how it was used to pass messages between people who were in captivity or long distances away from each other. It has not changed in hundreds of years nor has the value of music diminished in the eyes or culture of people all over the world. From ancient times, deep in jungles, through world wars and right up to present day, music has always been a perfect and camouflage way of communicating with people. American society has once again picked and chosen the type of music it saw fit to discriminate against due to its content and flare for violence. The music I am talking about is Rap Music.

Once a way to communicate effectively to the African American or black public all of the trials and tribulations of everyday life, now rap music has transformed into bragging about who has the most money and can act the most ignorant and embarrass your community the worst. Personally, rap music used to express how things were going for black people in their ghetto or neighborhood or how the police were pinpointing them daily about drugs or crime but the harsh reality is all rap music does is show racist white folks how foolish black people can become when they have a lot of money. Does this represent all rap music and its artist, definitely not, but the vast majority of rappers have gone down the wrong path? Rap music was an art of pure expression during a time when we as a black society had very few avenues to tell our story. Unfortunately, now rap music no longer tells a story but extravagantly destroys any credibility young artist coming out of bad circumstances used to elegantly depict for American society. One form of this rap music is so graciously referred to as "Gangster Rap".

"Gangster Rap" demonstrates the worse thing a society can represent or demonstrate about itself. In this kind of rap music, drug dealing, womanizing, stealing, murder and other negative elements are elevated to an acceptable status and praised. I fail to understand how this kind of dramatization would help any cause or movement in a positive way? In fact, all this kind of rap music does is lay out the plan of what has happened and what will happen later, exactly what lessor black men and women do in already dangerous neighborhoods. Not exactly the smartest or most efficient way to remain under the radar or to operate without the police getting in your business or knowing how and why you are doing what you are doing. This flashy and descriptive music only elevates the most negative things about black people. Feeding fuel to the fire of racism and societal mistrust of black people in general. Like I mentioned earlier, white society still only sees you as a lowly black person who once was a slave and is far beneath white people in every way.

What happened to the outreach and progress "Rap Music" or "Story Telling" provided to the Black community in a positive way? Where did the love and deep personal sentiment this descriptive and lesson building music go? I can tell you exactly where it went, into the hands of a younger and instantly gratifying generation out for only recognition and worship. All the kinds of negative things the black community does not need or want as a representation of the black community. We are not moving forward and have no basis or foundation to stand on when it comes to "Rap Music" in its' present day form. Once again, I am not talking about all the Rappers in the music industry, I am talking about the kind of Rappers who use this music to inform society about their financial status and number of women they can sleep with in a day, week, month or year. Unfortunately, I will not be looked upon positively for this point of view but it is important to understand the entire story and all the ways it is being helped or directly misrepresented.

The Rap community would be one of the most effective ways of communication and a great source of knowledge and unification if taped as an influential resource. Unfortunately, the number of followers who love "Rap Music" is rather huge and the Rappers maintain large amounts of financial status and recognition. If Rappers went back to way of expressing positive ideas and images in their songs, do you think the following would be as large as it today? Seriously, even if half of the listeners still followed these Rappers and were hearing positive words and ideas, positivity would spread like the plague and begin to help us as a Black Community gather some true understanding of what it is going to take to make change. I just do not see the Rap Industry as a positive influence on our younger generations nor is it moving any positive message forward. Just one more thing destroying society today and any forward momentum black people might be moving towards.

FIRST BLACK EVER!

If I hear one more time that any event was the first time a black man or woman accomplished something, I am going to go postal on America! Black people have been in America for as long as it has been created and due to many unfortunate events like slavery, racism, pure ignorance, dedicated bigotry and stupidity, our people continue to break through barriers year after year. Specific barriers black people were left out of for no more reason than we could be left out of the activity. I am not just talking about Sports but I will be talking about that later. The fact is that a lot of "Firsts" for black people were never a first but a cover up from White America. How would it look if a black man or woman created something or discovered anything of value in a place supposedly dominated by white people who think they are the center of our universe? I believe hatred and jealousy would overcome their stupidity and they would lose the right to remain the most dangerous and destructive entity on earth. An entity responsible for more death and destruction than ever other culture combined and doubled. So, you can imagine my dismay every single time a milestone or discovery by a black person is broadcasted across the Television when we already know originally, this milestone has just been previously covered and claimed by somebody without "black" in their title.

A poor man walks into a bar and claims he has discovered a way to turn dirt into food that is edible and immediately available for mankind's consumption.

This poor man has worked his entire life on this project and did not possess vast amounts of money to make this happen, even though he is the creator, developer and originator of the idea and process. Do you think in America, a black man will get any credit for the creation of this ground-breaking accomplishment? The group of people with the right amount of money and power will take over this product and make it their own, even if they make the actual creator disappear off the face of the earth. Do you think it mattered what timeframe we are talking about, early 1600s or present day? Many groundbreaking inventions of our time were the result of somebody you will never hear of due to the forces of dominance and ego centric views of society ran by racist, liars and thugs.

I know you have heard or seen the words, "For Whites Only" well this phrase had multiple meanings throughout history and still does to a certain instant. Not only was this horrible and embarrassing phrase for black and white people used in America but also spilled over into the business practices. Can you name the person who created the Street Light and who actually got rich from its' creation? I am not going to provide you with information you can get from reading a book but you will be interesting in the fact that they were not the same color. For a matter of fact, they were not even the same race. Do you have any idea who developed the ability to transport blood and the many kinds of ways it is stored? You would once again be surprised to see the color of this man and the color of the people who got rich from it. When White America is not seen as the al knowing and all controlling force, do you think they will allow anybody else to receive credit for anything more than being a footstool for White America's progress?

When you hear in the News, excluding "Fox News" because they do not care about anybody but white people and make racist statements daily, a black person has become the first CEO of an organization it was due to the organization allowing this black person to be the first black CEO. Do you think the actual black person who was hired as the first CEO was the first qualified black person to be CEO, no my friend? The only reason this black person became CEO is because the powers that be were either pressured or they had no choice but to give this black person a try due to a lower market value. If everybody is not available to participate, the win is considered hollow and unsatisfying! When a black person wins, you can rest assure the entire population was searched time and time again before reaching the pedestal. When a white person wins, they were destined to win and only go against a few other white people in general. Basically, making the odds for any white person tenfold over any other race whatsoever. Do you see what I am trying to say or since you already knew this already, are the clouds you have lived in your entire life parting and the sky suddenly parting ways?

When I said, "Black people have been in this Country as long as White people" that is exactly what I meant! It does not matter if we were slaves and stripped of everything all at once and made to serve a white master who wanted nothing more than economic profit and laziness to go hand and hand, the fact remains black people have always been here. This fact makes it hard and slaps me in the face when I hear a black person has done something for the first time in the year 2000 or later. What the hell is going on and are you kidding me? Black people are the reason a great many things were created and still are making it easier for America to do many of the things it still does to this day. We even had our hand in warfare long before Aristocratic Generals who received most of the training and discipline from other countries claimed creation of multiple tactics and techniques. How would it look if a black man showed a white man how to fight and survive when this country first began, I guarantee they would have killed him before any word reached any leadership?

I just do not want to ever hear a black person did something for the first time in America when we all know it is just the first time, white America has acknowledged it formally. It is so easy to keep down a race and continue to do so when you allow them to write the history books in your image and society. Could it be the threat of failing prior to a black person strikes fear in your heart? The last time I remember, diseases strike us all the same, bullets do not choose who to kill, or blood is the same color and consistency as yours and our hearts want the same thing. How is it that I am such a threat to you and your dominance? Let's talk about your raise to power!

ABSOLUTE MISTREATMENT OF BLACK PEOPLE

The multitude of feelings and shocking amazement welling up from within my heart fails into comparison of how African slaves were treated in America. Remember, I am not a rich superstar or Sports figure writing a book through somebody else, I am the average African American who works hard for a living and keeps his eyes open. What kind of person woke up one morning and decided to enslave people from a race, the entire race was NOT enslaved, and do the worst atrocities known to man with no regret or no mercy? On top of that, how could this same evil race of people enslave another race of people they did not know, did not care about and claim religious beliefs led them to make this decision? Call me ignorant, call me crazy but I know in my heart that evil fueled this action and the fact that an entire Nation thought this was acceptable completely incinerates my wellbeing and sealed rage. It is almost like we forgot or never learned of our past and try to live our lives with blinders to the rear and the sides. I am the strong-minded kind of person who cannot forget or forgive this evil and never will I accept it as the Birth of our Nation! You can go to Hell and take your History with

you!

I have heard the stories and true accounts about how African slaves were given up by African tribes who captured them during wars from other tribes and had no use for them. Does this make it right in the mind of any living and humane person to accept people as gifts and use them in any way they see fit? I

cannot think of any religion, excluding religions who used sacrifice as an

acceptable means, that do not preach caring for one another and making each

other stronger regardless of how one looks. As society still does to this day,

relentless and disturbed people interpret many representations of Script in the

way best allowing them to achieve their goals. Simply stated, "If the meaning of

anything is not what we need or want, it is understandable to change the content

to fit the new and improved version." How do you think slave owners slept at

night using religious beliefs to justify slavery and torture on a daily basis?

Am I to understand past Presidents owned slaves and plantations before

Slavery was abolished? The institution of the Presidency is still a viable option

in the United States of America so does that mean Slavery can also be a viable

option if not for the "Thirteenth Amendment" added to our "Constitution"? I am

living in a Country only one step from bringing back the institution of Slavery if

it really wanted to do so? I am sure If you looked at our governmental system

you might be very surprised on what laws are still an option. It took a President

who owned slaves himself to release the institution of Slavery when the

government he ran was divided on the subject due to Capitalist gain and pure

laziness? Why do you think I should feel sorry for the people who died fighting

in a war based on the institution of Slavery? A ridiculous war fought between

two sides of the United States of America on the grounds of letting an entire race of innocent people go free or stay in slavery and keep producing economic gain for a fat and lazy race of brutal people. A slow tear drops from my eye every time I think of how each man, woman and child were born into slavery and died with shackles on their feet, not knowing anything but the institution of Slavery.

Who was the initial person who made the decision to accomplish and sustain the act and institution of Slavery? I know there is a brutal, disgusting, white and immoral, fat and lazy, sorry ass individual who thought it would be acceptable to destroy an unwilling people and herd them like cattle. Bring these unsuspecting people over on boats with harsh conditions accepting if over 50 percent of them survived the long and brutal trip to the "Colonies" of America to be enslaved and work for free. I wish the ability to pin point the actual person was available but like the cover up of how slavery began and was maintained I am sure those records have been destroyed.

Another incredible story revolves around the first true and legal slave owner in America being a freed black indentured servant named Anthony Johnson. Here is how America tries to develop a story completely undermining the fact in the year 1618 African people were brought to the "Colonies" as slaves. Legally, since "indentured servants" which included African people who were brought over could only be held seven years and then released into freedom, the story of the first slave owner legally was a freed black indentured servant who later owned his own 250-acre farm in which he legally owned 25 African slaves. The reason Anthony Johnson is listed as the first slave owner in America is due to a dispute he had with a slave he officially owned and tried to leave by getting a job with a white man in a free state. Anthony Johnson took the legally owned slave named John Casor to court in North Hampton and demanded John Casor be his slave indefinitely. Since this was the first claimed case according to Colonial records in 1655, the claim is that this is the first legal claim of any slave in court making Anthony Johnson the first slave owner and John Casor the first legally owned slave. Unfortunately, the 40 plus years prior to this court case and claim of the first owned African slave being owned by a free black man was filled with African slaves living the horror of Slavery as a full institution with White Slave owners. You can dress it up any way you want, the fact remains Slavery destroyed the lives of millions of black people and racist white slave owners who felt it was acceptable.

How did we get to such a low point in human existence? Once again, who was the first person in the year 1618 to architect the idea to take other human lives and be so savage, brutal, immoral and deadly? Am I being judgmental about an entire part of American history I never experienced? YES, I am being the judge, jury and executioner. I cannot imagine when the idea of enslaving people for economic gain was proposed, every person in the room agreed and pushed this topic. It still makes me sick to my stomach to imagine the day and hour the lives of millions of people due to their skin color and origin were chosen to be desecrated on such a huge scale. Did they really think they had the Divine right to be GOD and make life decisions for any race or people? These are the things I wish I could gather information and find the person or persons who decided this was a good thing. Whether these racist and despicable white people knew it or not, they started a set of events we as black people are still feeling the effects from even today.

UNWARRANTED PORTRAYAL

The real portrayal of black people on television is alarming, racist and unfortunately the way white America saw us as a people. Obviously early television did not allow black people to appear on the silver screen because black people were still considered beneath the white experience. Black people are much too inferior to own televisions and should be outside working in some fashion were the thoughts of white America. Or, black people were used as props in movies such as slaves or servants or maids. The proper and only way white America saw black people. To experience this fact, watch movies made in the early 1930s to 1950s where black people were completely missing or used in a negative and demeaning role. Later, black people experienced more success on television with a few black pioneers who made it possible for black people to show their talent. In the present day, black people are headlining movies and pulling millions to the box offices and on television making black people all over the world proud of all their accomplishments. With these facts in mind, I am now going to tell you what I have seen on television for many years as a black man in the year 2014.

I am concerned about two things when it comes to watching television and being a black person, why are black people portrayed negatively almost always and why do most television shows always have one black "Token" who has a small part at best? Let me start off by introducing Police shows like "Cops" and

"First 48" known for portraying black people as the kind of people who must be the only individuals committing crimes in America. The simple fact is more Police calls are directed at white people who by the way outnumber non-white people 10 to one in most American cities. Another simple fact revolves around white people not getting arrested and given any warning when they clearly have done things warranting arrest by the Police. When the same kind of crime or disturbance is registered by a white and a non-white person, 75 percent of the time the non-white person is arrested based on nothing but the color of their skin. No wonder such a high percentage of black people are in jail serving hard time on the average of 10 plus years longer than the same crime by a white person. Not only are black people portrayed as criminals but sentenced as criminals at a much higher rate regardless of circumstances. On a personal level, I have been pulled over by the Police and found it funny how thoroughly my credentials were scrutinized and when I was in a vehicle with one of my white friends how quickly they were given a warning for the same offense. If this is the way America has been portraying black people on television Police shows, no wonder why the Police have been profiling them more and more.

Emotional, terrifying, comedic, and realistic television shows produce entertainment value while undermining and degrading black people year in and year out. First, how is a television show about the entertainment industry of music portraying the worst thing money does to black people considered anything positive to anybody? This show which will remain nameless includes members of the entertainment industry with excessive amounts of money degrading women, who by the way most of the time are ex strippers, acting very inappropriately and putting their personal business for all of America to see and create negative opinions about. Opinions about this show only create the racist and negative view of black people in America and what happens when large amounts of money are earned and spent on purely negative and stupid things or people. Predominately white television shows for the most part portray unrealistic views of white people that are acceptable and not negative. When these same white television shows want to add any negative element, a black person is introduced and portrayed negatively. When a black person is the main character in a predominately white television show, they are mostly portrayed as an individual cheating with a white man, running from the law, fucking up in a major way until they are saved by a white person, created for doing a negative thing or showing how a black person has the hardest life and cannot keep it together without major sacrifice. For every black person who is portrayed as anything positive on television there are 100 portrayed in one of the ways previously described! It is not enough for black people to be portrayed negatively but the fact black people are portrayed at all on television.

WOMEN AND DEGRADABLE ALLOWANCE

I could not be more disgusted when I think of the portrayal of black women in a society who has always regarding them as pieces of meat used by every race due to the history of black people in general. Why does the world continue to automatically think negatively when black people are put into any equation? Slavery has permanently marked the past and future of black people and people of all races continue to treat black people accordingly. As for the black woman who was brutally raped, used for breeding, picked and segregated for sexual entertainment and gave birth to the Malato black people who are much lighter skinned than original African slaves. In many characteristics, there has not been much change to the treatment of black women in our present society but not always due to white society for the most part. Some black women are strong, proud, dominance in most families and continue to uplift the black women in society. Other black women continue to provide evidence of the mistreatment and derogatory ways black women suffered during slavery and beyond. Several examples of this can be seen in our unfortunate culture of so called black people who think they are successful in society.

Why does a black woman think she has made it or is successful because she exploits herself posing half naked or dancing around half naked in a rap video? This kind of exploitation of black women self-inflicted by both black men and women show in detail the negative connotations once put upon black women during slavery. In rap videos and half naked pictures, black women are being used for nothing more that entertainment and is being degraded in the worse way. Some may call this artistic expression but do you really see this as anything more than merely for entertainment? When I watch rap videos which display the black women as a piece of meat for all of society to see, I feel deep down in my stomach how far away this is from the treatment of black women during slavery. Obviously, in rap videos black women are not being raped or beat but most seem to be unhappy and end up being treated as nothing more than a party favor. Which then leads to what you have read in some books written by video vixens or women who are in rap videos that they are raped, treated like property and degraded horribly. Why would a black woman or any woman allow themselves to be treated in the same way as black women were treated during the long 400 plus years of slavery?

The porn industry which is an institution that is well known for degrading all races of women and a lot of men also contributes to the degradation of black women even though these black women are volunteering to perform these sexual acts for money. Did you know one of the highest sells in pornography is a black woman having sex with a white man or men? This form of pornography is called interracial pornography but we all know why it is one of the best sellers, it is the representation of what happened to black women during the institution of slavery. African slave women being brutally raped and chosen for reproduction by white slave masters. If you do not see the connection, why is this form of pornography one of the best sellers worldwide? White people and most of society truly believe this form of pornography is correct and white men should be dominating and having rough sex with black women whether they want to or not. Degradation is only the beginning of what happens to these black women, the biggest black stars in pornography are also the black women who participate mostly if not completely in interracial pornography scenes. Closet racist are the first people to comment on this kind of interracial pornography relaying the message that all black women need to be dominated by white men and treated like the dogs they represent. Regardless if you believe in this being remotely related to slavery, read an earlier chapter of this book and compare interracial pornography with the institution of slavery and how black woman were treated daily.

Do beautiful and talented black women need to use sex appeal to cover up the fact that maybe they do not possess any talent at all but a sexy body? Performers of the past and present have used sex appeal to promote themselves into the limelight without having an ounce of talent. Why do black women feel this is the only way to stay relevant in the mainstream of entertainment? A beautiful singing voice and lovely dress were all that was necessary to sell records in an industry known for pure talent. Well, performers of today are not only using black women to sell sex in videos and magazines but these same black women are using their bodies to sell an image not associated with talent. Society almost expects a black woman who sings and makes videos to expose herself to keep you thinking about her regardless if the music she is making is worthy of a second thought. I can think of a lot of singers who need to continue doing this due to their talent being on the lower side of things. What happen to the singers who I will not name who could sing the "National Anthem" flawlessly or make a video with nothing but pictures, a microphone and beautiful makeup and still go Platinum every time? These days are gone due to a Society that expects black women to exaggerate the obvious and use sex to sell their product. Do you really think "wardrobe malfunctions" really exist or are they all preplanned and known to keep you thinking about them for years later? The answer to that kind of question is painfully obvious and unfortunate. This kind of behavior will never ensure the progress of erasing negative thoughts about black women or black people in society.

It is bad enough black women are considered lower on the totem pole than black men but the necessity of degrading themselves to make a buck or move up the corporate ladder continues to make us fall behind even further in society. Black people will never be able to erase slavery and the treatment of black women from their minds but we as a people need to make better and more effective decisions about life. Black women need to stop being exploited by society regardless if it is by black men in a certain industry or white men in another. The reality is black women have become very powerful and very influential in this world but for every woman who is successful, another 100 or more are doing negative things making black people be scrutinized harshly.

UNFORTUNATE BLACK EXAMPLES

Constantly society continues looking for ways to make successful and powerful black athletes the objects of scrutiny and disaster. I am not here to name names or even give details but I would like to see our black professional athletes seen and respected in a more positive light. But this light can only be achieved when black professional athletes decide to act and portray themselves as role models for all of people who watch, idolize and immolate them daily. It is not just about the endorsements, money and notoriety but the true influence and power black professional athletes have in the limelight and do not even realize it. Can black professional athletes add anything positive to the movement and struggle black people have in this white society? Yes, professional black athletes have an incredible amount of power and have been destroying it by acting inappropriately in the public eye. What in the hell are you thinking when you know you are being watched with a fine-toothed comb and still make ignorant decisions that will eventually catch up with you? There are a lot of examples of this stupidity but my purpose in this chapter is to expose the reality of how much harm these negative outcomes and circumstances are making things much harder for black people to progress forward in a white society.

Besides the fact when anything negative happens to a professional black athlete it is amplified and dragged across media at an alarming rate, the circumstances are usually of the worse kind possible. First example comes from a black professional athlete who decided it would be better to commit adultery over and over when he had a wonderful family and beautiful children to go home to daily. He thought it would be better to go out and sleep with as many hookers and porn stars as humanly possible. And what did you think the media immediately did to this professional black athlete? They destroyed him from the inside out and not a person who watches television or listens to the radio did not know about his situation and how horrible the world now thought of him. Even though all of the circumstances were a part of his private and personal life, the media saw two things they could exploit, the fact he was a professional black athlete and he was married to a white woman. The biggest two reasons, the media felt it could destroy this professional black athlete with little effort. Unfortunately, the negative media attention not only took the perfect limelight this professional black athlete had built but portrayed him as an example of the typical professional black athlete. Once again, another way racism is amplified in the media and in white society. Do you really believe, he was the only professional athlete who cheated on his wife and was caught? No, he was a professional black athlete in a predominately white sport which he was dominating and the media now had ammunition to cut him down and turn his limelight into a negative thing. Thus, showing how negativity is never a positive thing and can be exploited harshly especially if a professional black athlete is involved.

Professional black athletes are looked upon by white society as demons or cursed individuals who once were slaves and luckily made it to the big time. I know those words seem a little harsh but think about the reality of how many sports excluded black athletes until recent decades. As far as I am concerned, most of the records in the record books for most if not all sports are false due to nothing but white people participation. As soon as non-white people broke into professional sports through the efforts of brave black men and women, all records should have had asterisks placed next to them with white only tags. White people had no problem making signs labeled "White Only" and placing them on businesses so why not on all professional sports records prior to non-white involvement?

Domestic violence invokes the worst feelings and sentiments towards the individual considered the perpetrator. When black professional athletes are accused of domestic violence, their image is tarnished beyond recognition. Not only does white America treat any professional athlete as a demon but all of America will participate due to the truths about domestic violence. Fact, no man should put their hands on a woman out of anger or cause bodily harm on a woman who cannot protect herself. I, along with a majority of people in America believe this to be true and when a professional black athlete commits this crime and it is exemplified in the media, it gives America a hurtful and animalistic image of black people in general. Do you think black people look animalistic in a society that already regards them as animals? Black people need to stop fueling

the fire by making bad choices such as domestic violence either as a professional

black athlete or a normal person who works to keep his family's American dream

a reality. Unfortunately, the millions of people who follow professional athletes

see only what the media wants them to see and in the case of the black

professional athlete it is negative especially when these athletes are highly

popular and successful. As I mentioned before, anytime the media can bring

down the credibility of a professional black athlete, it is done with pin point

accuracy. Not the role models we want our children to look up to in any way,

shape or form.

Unfortunately, the most popular athletes around the world pull the most

headlines daily and regardless of their race but only the professional black

athletes are scrutinized beyond reproach. There have been times professional

athletes have committed the same crimes in a familiar timeframe. Who do you

think received the most attention and was followed closely from beginning to

end? The professional black athlete was followed for more than 8 weeks and

even beyond to ensure society saw the outcome of the trail and the consequences

of criminal action in professional sports. The other athlete who was white, was

hardly covered and to this day, unless you read about it specifically on Yahoo or

in past news coverage, it is hard to determine what the crime might have been or

the outcome of the trail. All in all, the media who was sprung from a white background and specifically looks out for white society continues to use negative news towards non-white people as a method of bringing down or shedding negative light on all races besides their own. Will society ever feel the need to acknowledge the kind of legacy they are leaving for the children of all races to continue to be separate and not equal?

ASSIMILATION

When I think of the word 'assimilate' a very rigid chill comes over my bones and I begin to pray black people will have nothing to do with such a thing. But as I come to the realization of how messed up our world has become and the need to not make waves in an already turbulent ocean is the safest way to live peacefully. Do you believe any historical figure who caused change on a profound scale thought for one second they would assimilate with their surroundings to not be noticed? When anything or anybody assimilates, either by force or due to emanate threat, they lose or replace their soul with another person. As described in a previous chapter how I wanted slave owners and slaves to switch souls, when you assimilate into a society or area, the years of life you experienced were for nothing and all the lessons you learned are gone into existence. Unfortunately, assimilation is one of the biggest tools black people who become very successful use to counteract the fact they are black people in a white society.

I am a 48-year old black man who has attended college, served in the Armed Forces and now write what I feel based on my environment and how I see it from my own point of view. If I sell 500,000 copies of this book and become very successful, would it be right to assimilate myself into society and lose my insight on how society treats black people? This is how I see assimilation and how successful black people see it as well; however, the only thing accomplished by assimilation into a society that sees you as a negative character is keeping your enemy closer for blame and scrutiny. If I was on the inside of the firing box instead of the target, maybe I can get away from racism and the pure hatred most white people have for black people in general. Not the case, white people will always think of black people as slaves and far beneath them regardless of your status or holdings in society, in simple terms, you are still black in their eyes. Assimilation into a society that hates you effects other people besides yourself and I am going to tell you why?

For every Uncle Tom who feels it is important to change their appearance, their clothes, the way they talk, or the place they live is the ultimate disrespect to every black slave and black person working hard to establish their identity in this highly white society. When I mean "Uncle Tom" this refers to the individual slave who decided to do whatever the white man said and sell out his black brothers to gain personal conveniences while other African slaves were beaten or killed due to them being a snitch and a person without loyalty. Is it necessary to sell out your race to accomplish a few things that you are not accomplishing? You think assimilating and acting in such a manner you seem white to society. You are black, African American, a negro and the lowest form of person in America regardless of what you may possess or think. You feel the need to show your children who are also black people, it is acceptable to leave their culture behind and be the person who is unrecognizable in the mirror. Nobody is asking you to wear an African Tribal ceremonial gown but to be the black person you were prior to you earning a better status in society. You are the kind of person other black people need as a role model, we all know most of our rich people are not acting as any kind of role model you would want your kids to look up to or copy. I have heard the phrase, "More money creates more problems," and I would like to change the words to, "More money creates unrecognizable people." Assimilation reminds me of a dead man walking because everything on the inside is gone and what remains is just an empty shell.

The original question I ask was, "Why do black people want to assimilate into a white society?" Money and power are two good reasons as well as cover and concealment from racism. The reason might be good in their eyes but the situation never changes in the eyes of American white society. Case in point, a black man who has struggled for years trying to make it big in entertainment or music or business, finally manages to gain fame and fortune. Prior to his gaining fame and fortune, he believed in the struggle of black people in America and the way society sees black people in general. He would participate in black businesses and donate money and his time to the progress of the African American person in America. Clothes and materialistic things were not an issue and he spoke with an ethnic tone but still sounded well educated. This was all prior to him becoming very successful and massing a large amount of money and status.

Amazingly enough, here is the status of the same black person who become a success story in America after becoming successful. The first thing you will notice about the increase in money and status is the way he reacts to the "Black Situation" he now calls it. He does not believe he is one of the black people he used to hear about who has racial issues in American society. There is a profound thought of acceptance among other rich people who are mostly white and do not stand for ignorance. Black people are now criminals and he will not live in the same neighborhood as them and feels like he needs to protect his assets on another level.

At this point in his life the full and unchangeable transformation into a pseudo white person has taken place and for him, there is no turning back. Even if he lost his riches and became a very poor and broke person, he would rather take his own life than admit he was wrong and recognize his mistakes. I guess turning your back on your culture due to money, fame and success is the American way for cowards and uncultured black people. Unfortunately, when a black person does reach fame and success on such a high level, the first thing they want to call themselves are more cultured and refined, but realistically, the only thing that really happened was the complete and ultimate reduction of what little culture they had left. A simple answer to a simple question, yes, black people will assimilate into an unrecognizable human being due to the addition of wealth, fame and success. Plain and simple!!!

IGNORANCE

If I was stopped on the street and ask what has been the most destructive force on this earth historically, I would have to answer with the word "Ignorance." Ignorance has been the mainstay and driving force enabling cultures to be destroyed or conquered. Ignorance justified the creation and at the same time destruction of a Nation and a people. It might be hard to explain how ignorance has played such an important role in the development of society but it stands to be the driving force. Ignorance of any culture makes way for the ignorance of another culture to rule and sometimes destroy the original culture. Put simply, if I lay trust in somebody I do not know and they realize this fact, it will become easy to do negative things to me before I understand what is going on. This describes our world and our present state of society.

Did the Native Americans think the people who arrived in ships were going to nearly eradicate their entire culture and kill millions of their people all while showing real hospitality? Not only did these people not discover the New World which was inhabited by Native Americans hundreds of years prior to them arriving, they claimed it in the name of their respective Country. Interesting, if I decided to sail on a ship and land on Hawaii but saw it was inhabited but wanted it for myself, what would be my best option to not disappoint my King? Yes, claim I discovered the new land and kick everybody else off by any means necessary. This is exactly what happened when these people landed on an already inhabited land. They were literally trained by the Native Americans with cooking methods and preservation, medicine and hunting ability and then the actual killing of Native Americans began. These people wasted no time in hunting, deceiving, spreading unknown diseases and destroying the culture of the Native Americans in quick order. Ultimately, declaring war on the Native Americans and forcing them to live on Indian Reservation.

The ignorance depicted in the situation between Native Americans and these other people is very easy to see because Native Americans trusted white people and were nearly eradicated due to their ignorance of these people. Not only did white people smile in the faces of the Native Americans and preach peace, they accepted their knowledge and teachings before pulling the wool over their eyes and literally destroying them from within. All in the name of a country they were fleeing from themselves due to unfair conditions of all kinds including types of slavery and servitude and allegiance to a King. Interesting how events come full circle. Ignorance allowed white people to fool, destroy and claim the land for themselves.

Did African tribes who possessed captured warriors, women and children realize the travesty they would bring upon their own people or did ignorance and greed drive them into trading people for products like spices and clothing? It was not like white people went to Africa and other places and took by force black people to work in the New World or America under the institution of Slavery.

The Africans who were acquired by white people early in the history of America were the product of wars leftover people who were not killed but traded for other products by African Kings. These people happen to be African and had no choice or say in anything that was going to happen to them in the future, either death or be traded. What white people did to black people is just one of the most prolific horrible treatments of a people in a Nation that was founded and brought about on the backs of these very same African or black people. The African tribes who traded these captured African people were ignorant to the atrocities and treatment their virtual brothers would receive in America.

Is ignorance the driving force fueling the unfortunate human notion of conquering and enslaving another or different race of people for amusement or entertainment? Is it necessary for other races to destroy cultures that could have been used as a learning tool for future benefit? No, it is easier for people, regardless of color to destroy, plunder for riches and cover up their mess by enslaving or wiping out the conquered race. There have been several races of people and cultures wiped out due to wide spread gold and rich culture rumors. The Mayans and Aztecs were two very powerful Nations who existed long before the Spanish and English people sought them out due to legends of gold and riches and destroyed the culture permanently. These cultures were more than just rich with Gold but laid the footprints down for how societies should be structured, math, calendars, preserving history, art and a valley of other informational knowledge nearly destroyed due to ignorance and greed.

I believe the entire world could have progressed further and more quickly without the destruction of ancient cultures and legend due to ignorance, greed and the human evil constant. Working together instead of working to destroy others should have been the mainstay of history, unfortunately conquering and enslavement have been the dominant option. It does not matter where in history you look, there has always been a people being enslaved, eradicated, mistreated and murdered due to the advancement of another race. This is highly unfortunate and destructive within any society and only leads to long lasting unruly sentiment and mistreatment. Horrible events happening many years ago are still being felt through the passing of knowledge and existence of that people and culture. America is one of the best examples of this kind of treatment of a people and the knowledge that racism against black people may never change or be stopped.

MEDIA'S UNFAIR COVERAGE

I would be remiss to put the media and anything positive in the same book regarding its continued negative coverage of anything not the color white or wealthy. When it comes to media coverage and the Nation we live in, if it is not white, it is not right. The only time the media covers anything not white, it is a guarantee it will be positively negative about another race, especially black. When a child goes missing and there are plenty of children that go missing daily, you can believe in your heart, if it is a white child from a wealthy family, media coverage will automatically follow. If the child is any other race unless the family is of superstar or super rich status, the media will not even blink an eye. This fact has been tested and proven several times over and in several instances. The best thing the Media is good at doing is ensuring minorities are covered in the most negative light as possible daily. If you have heard the rhetoric regarding how the Media will intentionally pick out the worst minority individual it can find for an interview, it is very true. The consistent negativity displayed towards minorities by the Media is something that has been going on for a long time unfortunately. With a powerful advantage over media and the coverage of everyday life, black people turning to the media for any reason is almost a waste of time for forward progress in society.

Opposition to the fact media is one of the most racist and ludicrous foundations for any race except white has been explored and argued. The media claims minorities put themselves in the most negative situations and all the media does is cover the news as they see it. This might be true if they covered anything positive about minorities and covered anything negative about white people. Case in point, the only reason the media gets involved with cases involving a black man being killed is because a white man committed the act and the situation holds controversy. Any time the media can cover a black man being killed by a white man and somehow the white man is exonerated through white justice, this is another way to make white America seem as if the clocks are rolled back during a time when killing black folks was legal and encouraged. And for some reason, the coverage for any situation as previously mentioned occurs, you can guarantee the coverage will be long and every news station will find ways to argue how the white man was in his legal rights to kill a black man. Not going to mention any names but FOX News is a professional at being one sided and bilaterally racist. Sorry but it is the truth.

When searching online for as many cases involving black men in jail for life who were charged and barely proven or justified in the self-defense death of a white man, you would be shocked at the small number of the same incidents involving white men in the same predicament. The only difference now is the media who systematically ensures society sees only the white man and every reason under the sun why he is innocent regardless of the true nature of the case is intriguing. Unfortunately, this is a battle that we cannot or will not win if the media is so uneven with its coverage of the races. Why is it every time a Black Panther rally which are minimal due to the toxicity of the government and the almost eradication of the Movement by the Government, it is called a racist action even though they are protesting not only black rights but the rights of every person from black to white and everything in between. But when a Ku Klux Klan rally is televised and of course hidden far away from the public eye because they are a bunch of gutless cowards, the media never says a thing about how racist this extremely racist faction is and always has been. In fact, the media damn near roots them on and encourages their actions in the public eye. Once again ensuring white people regardless of their capacity are lifted and positively portrayed in the public eye and black people are not.

Did you know the media is still covering the kidnapping and murder of a little white girl who has been gone for over a decade and still cannot cover a little black or Latina girl kidnapped a few days ago? Is it just me or is the reality of the media so lopsided in its coverage of white to minority children it makes you want to throw your hands in the air and just wonder. Could the harsh reality of it all be the progression of white people is so strong and dominant minorities do not stand a chance? I see life as a precious thing regardless of how the media or America sees it. Equality was promised to all and I do not think I have ever seen it in any circumstance, and that my friend is and always will be a major problem. Media coverage of any kidnapped child is a huge advantage and could result in the capture and return of the child regardless of race or color. If the media did not see this as a race game, society would not continue to be the backwards, white, racially motivated and negative society we presently live. All life matters and all situations should be covered equally and sufficiently.

Once upon a time a comedian who is black and a national spokesman who is white were both caught up in a major investigation regarding alleged rape and alleged child molestation. For months, the media has covered the comedian and scrutinized every movement and monstered his life into a world wind of negativity and destruction of his legacy. So far as to reach so far back into his life to a time when none of us were even born. Highly publicized and highly scrutinized has been the media's main function so far as to practically giving the comedian no choice but to leave the United States for safety and life continuation. On the other hand, the white national spokesman who allegedly committed crimes just as bad or worse has had little media coverage and little attention in the media. How can this be? How can atrocities be committed by a white man and not be covered as vigorously by the media? Oh, here is your answer to this very complex but simple question, the National Spokesman is WHITE! If he was a black man, the coverage would be never ending and the destruction of his legacy would come into questions more times than you can count. But obviously, unless you follow the news closely, I have a feeling you probably cannot even name the national spokesman I am referring to in this paragraph. Just like the many serial killers who are all white except for one or the Catholic Priest who decided to molest young boys and get away with it for the most part. If any of these individuals or criminals had been black, they would still be in the news to this very day. The discrepancy of media coverage between the races in any situation has spiraled out of control and should be addressed and corrected.

LAUGHING IS THE BEST MEDICINE AND A TEACHABLE MOMENT

Black comedians have and always will be a positive influence on black society by showing and depicting the actual lifestyles and daily journeys of how black and white people interact amongst one another. The same things rappers used to do until they decided to change what they rap about. Consequently, black comedians do this in a very amusing way, some with a lot of cussing and some without any cussing or using derogatory methods period. Teaching society the way the races communicate and either love or despise each other is a mission everyone should try and accomplish daily. Sit down and listen to a black comedian or a white comedian and you will get the climate of society through their eyes. Whether it is a mastery of using dummies to get the point across or physical comedy, the result is still the same. Female comedians have the luxury of depicting society from a race and a gender viewpoint.

Old school Black Comedians like Richard Pryor who is consequently one of my favorite comedians, explained through his comedy exactly how black people reacted to the actions of white people. His stand-up skits of how a white person would respond to a group of black people standing in line and looking at him and his wife was hilarious but at the same time showing the thoughts of society directed towards race relations. This skit showed how white people were intimidated and often afraid a group of black people were nothing but thugs and would commit crimes against the white people. Without realizing the teaching and knowledge Mr. Pryor was providing on social climate, the audience would simply laugh because it was funny. Richard Pryor was a black comedian in the early 70s-80s but his mastery of real life social and economic climates can still be a teaching aide for future generations of young people throughout the world. His elaboration of what black people do when they become rich by moving out of the old neighborhood and trying to become and sound white still holds true today and came far before anybody was thinking about this transformation.

Another black comedian who indirectly taught a generation of people in our Society of all races was Eddie Murphy. Not only did this black comedian teach our generation the true climate of races but also starred in movies that focused on race relations such as "Trading Places" and "Beverly Hills Cop." Two movies showing how different black and whites live and act towards one another. "Trading Places" especially showed how a black and white man could virtually live in one another's worlds and be interchangeable and unnoticed except for the color of their skin. This movie showed how success is not saved and ultimately pinpointed for only white people in America. An excellent example of how all people can live the American dream and nothing can hold you back. Except yourself. Eddie Murphy's comedy style focused on the existence and sometimes war between black and white people in general but in a funny way. His method of comedy is more direct on how black and people did not get along or were in the same boat and needed to get along or everybody was going down. And as Richard Pryor portrayed the relationship of the Police and black people, Eddie Murphy illustrated with words just how untrusting black people are when it comes to the Police and fairness and violence towards one another. A topic being harshly talked about by the entire world because of the atrocities and incidents occurring regularly.

Now let us talk about some white comedians who are doing the same thing with race relations in their acts unknowingly on a global scale. A white comedian who uses puppets to perform his act and has created not only a huge following here in America but also abroad due to his portrayal of a Muslim suicide bomber. Known for calling all people who are not Muslim, Infidels and a host of other names, this character used shows how society reacts and is nervous about seeing a potential terrorist due to his nationality and race. Even though, this character is just a funny attempt at being a terrorist and admits it openly. This character was banned in several countries due to his antics but the white comedian usually finds a way to present the character because he believes the world could learn a lot from a funny terrorist. The point hits home and is a wonderful teaching aide for the world. His other characters include a drunk hillbilly race car watching idiot, a black pimp, super hero, crazy Island guy and a Mexican Jalapeno. All from different racial elements of America joining together as one team and teaching the differences between race and their actions.

Lastly, a white female comedian has opened the eyes of America with her comedy based on female interaction within America and the racial climate from a women's point of view. Her recent Movie and comedy act depict her as a woman in comedy who thinks has it much harder due to her being a woman. She has worked hard and made it to the level of stardom other male comedians can only dream about. But her comedy includes her point of view on Hispanic always working and having a job and the brothers (black men) not having a job and talking loud in movie theaters during the movie. She is illustrating how society still sees minorities today and kind of does not care about race relations as much but still shows the tension is still present between the races. Her kind of nonchalant attitude about race is indicative of the fact racism remains but nobody is really acting on it and keeping it in the closet most of the time. Comedians of our day make jokes about having only one black friend and not hanging with them at their house because it would bring down the property value and get them kicked out of their circle of friends or family completely. These things are put in the context of comedy but show either directly or indirectly how the racial tones and climate are today.

BROTHERHOOD UNLIKELY

Do you need to use more than one hand to count the number of friends you possess of another race or nationality? I am going to be honest and admit, I do not need to use more than one hand or a couple fingers to answer that question! Why is that a fact among so many people in the United States or the world? Simply put, white people do not think they have anything in common with black people, Hispanic people do not think they have anything in common with Japanese people, I can go on and on with list of so called incompatible races but I would be lying. Our skin is made up of the same molecules and cells, our blood is blue when it is oxygenated and red when it spills onto the ground, our bones are made up of the same calcium and our brains are all use electrical synopsis to move information throughout our bodies. We are virtually the same except for the amount of information we learn and our actual physical sizes. What are some of the reasons why people feel it is necessary to stay among their own races when it comes to friendship and romance?

What is it going to look like to my family if I walk in my parent's home with a person who is not black? Now, I am speaking in general terms that do not represent myself but represent a large slice of America. Your parents are your only source of society until you reach out on your own but unfortunately you will follow their lead when it comes to racial and political views. Your family will most likely not like the fact you brought a person home who was not the same race as yourself. They will see it as you are breaking the code of the family in which only your race is acceptable and tolerated. This might not be the view of the individual person who is bringing the person of another race into their parent's home but is what is expected. If only the chain of racism could be broken prior to the child leaving the home, this type of thinking could be passed along to all the newer generation of that family. Like I have stated before and people know me to act like this regularly, I will not punish the child but only want to find the parents who put such negative points of view in the child's head to begin with. We are all products of our own personal socio and economic environment.

Is it possible for a wealthy and a poor person to be friends in America? Well, in America, wealthy and poor equates to white and black unfortunately. The same question is asked and answered in the previous paragraph but with a few minor changes. I happen to know of several wealthy black people, so what becomes of the excuse to not want to be friends with an opposite race at that situation? Racism takes over at that point and white people do what they have been doing since the time of slavery and be a true racist. Any white person over the age of 55 I do not trust in most cases because it likely they were on the fence chanting with the rest of the racist long ago when black people were first trying to protest racial equality. As previously stated much earlier in this book, these same people now must keep their racism in the closet or either be an open racist, something these same cowards will not do. You would think racism might lesson if people just worked together and came together the same way. Why is it so difficult for a white and a black person be good friends? I can tell you from personal experience it is more than possible and has been portrayed on television and in real life.

Everybody does not see color when it comes to people, wealth, dignity, ability and stature. Some people only see another person with individual qualities and abilities bread therein. Are you telling me only white people can make things work in society, business, life and love? You could not be further from the truth, so it stands very clear people of all races must have cooperated and worked together to make excellent accomplishments. Also meaning these very same people must have been and probably still are friends. You can only go so far with the notion white and black people generally do not get along. Education has jumped up and provided a clear and concise understanding of how it is possible and likely you will work or know people outside of your race. Do only white or only black people play any sport known today? Maybe that is how it was in the past but today, all sports are integrated, all schools are integrated, the military is integrated, there really is no option but for you to know and befriend somebody outside of your race. And it only makes good sense to do so.

Unless you live under a rock and in some backwards country of racial intolerance, if you answered with one or two friends of the opposite race, you have a major problem and am qualified to be a pure racist. Even "FOX News"

must incorporate itself with the opposite race from time to time between the

racist views it portrayed on television. When it really counts and people decide

they need each other, continues to be one of the only times people work together

without seeing each other's race. Unfortunately, this kind of situation only

presents itself far and few between. Bullets do not stop and decipher if a certain

race might be present before it kills an individual. A knife does not turn into

rubber because it is about to go into a white person and not a minority. I am very

confused on why people refuse to be friends with people of another race. A

black comedian name Paul Mooney put it best, "White people can find an alien,

feed him, let him live with them, eat their food but cannot live next to a black

person for two seconds." Enough said!!!

HISTORICAL AND INFORMATION DREAMS OF CRUELTY

Have you ever woken from the same horrifying dream night after night and realized somebody or something was trying to point you in a specific direction or motivate you to do something that might change the world? I truly believe I have been directed to write about the infinite observations of black people and help society get a clearer vision of how we have been treated present day and how the past has made this happen. When I look at a white person over the age of 50 and begin to receive a clear vision of where they were and who they were during the uprisings and major events that shaped the Civil rights movement of the past. Sometimes I can see them chasing black people down the street in the neighborhoods they grew up in or alongside other white people cursing black people for wanting equality. I looked in a very old white person's eyes and had a flashback of a horse and whip being sprung at slaves while they were picking cotton in a huge and very hot field with blistering hands and huge headaches from dehydration. I also felt as if the African slave I was looking at turned around and looked right into my eyes transferring all of the pain and torment accompanying slavery. These visions make me upset and want to retaliate on the spot but I figure in this society, I am only one punch away from 20 years of imprisonment, especially at this moment in time.

I sometimes look at historical pictures on a wall at a museum or in a book of black people who were slaves and suddenly have a shuttering feeling of unwillingness and anguish. I could literally see a vision of African slaves being beaten for the amusement of a crowd of fat, rich and lazy Southern plantation owners. I could feel how the African slaves were shuffled in one by one and the slave masters taking bets on who would yell the loudest while being beaten half to death and then forced to go back outside and work the rest of the day. African slaves were nothing more than entertainment and free labor to the United States for over 400 years. I am still trying to wrap my head around how it was attainable and moral to force another race of people to provide free slave labor while being treated so poorly they had to name the institution "Slavery". How could any black person or any person not feel a sense of ugliness and not want to throw up in a dirty garbage can over the institution of "Slavery"?

Where do you think the souls of the millions of African slaves have gone? I am hoping the souls of all the African slaves never left and are channeling the ultimate revenge against every racist white individual among us today. I have had this dream where somehow the negative energy of African slaves was absorbed by influential black people and used to strike a harsh and debilitating action against past, present and future white slave masters and their relatives. Interesting enough, most white people today who had relatives who were apart of slavery, know it and embrace it like an award. Is it just me or is that just as psychotic as it is racist? There is no true punishment worthy of reminding the world exactly what the United States did to become a nation and whose backs they stood upon but pay back is coming swift and hard.

Looking through the eyes of a slave is impossible, however, when I dreamed of such a thing, I was trying to figure out if was based off the movies and Television shows I have seen about slavery or the real thing? I am not claiming to have done such a thing but I think I came close. I dreamed I was looking out of the eyes of a African slave during the times of slavery and what I think I saw astonishes me as well as horrifies my soul. I saw African slaves being used for target practice daily while white slave owners made bets amongst each other. I saw African slaves being tied up to trees and used as punching bags and dart boards for the white, rich and immoral. My heart dropped out of my body when I saw how African slaves were used like dogs for fighting in which the winner was the one left alive and he would be hung for further entertainment after the fight was complete. I went so far as to see how African slave women were raped in front of their husbands by white slave masters over and over resulting in pregnancy of the now mulatto generation. How a white and wealthy man could buy slave women for only sexual favors until they finally killed them by burning them alive in barns or old abandoned houses. I want to say again how my dreams could be from what I have studied and watched on television but either way, I do feel a sense of passion about what I have seen and the feelings were not entirely mine at those moments.

I am not trying to write what you think I should or tone down my language for society but the fact that I am not a wealthy person or famous person, I thought I would tell the truth about how society truly sees black people. I did have a dream that explains famous black people in society. It referred to what was sized up as the "house negro" or "Uncle Tom" figure portrayed so accurately in novels. I saw rich and famous black people of today as these two previous kind of people during slavery. The ones who sang for the white man and danced for the white man with a huge cheese eating grin on their faces. The African slaves who were not on this level were outside doing the work and being destroyed from the inside out, physically, mentally and emotionally. This also explains in detail the differences in treatment between light skinned and dark skinned black people, but we will discuss that matter in a different area. African slaves who worked inside of the homes and worked parties and gatherings of the white household were accepted on a different level in society because they could be seen by white society and not from the end of a whip. In my opinion based on my dreams these are the entertainers of today and black people who think assimilation is a positive thing for themselves and their surroundings. Consequently, the way black people act when they become rich and famous or are chosen to be in the house possess a direct correlation.

I postulated through my incredibly vivid dreams and accurate study of African slave history the direct correlation between African slaves who worked inside the white master's house and black wealthy entertainers today. First, I want to assure you that every wealthy and black entertainer does not fall into this unfortunate category. What I am speaking of comes from the treatment of African slaves who worked in the white master's house. These African slaves who with lighter skin were treated with almost human like qualities. Their food was better, not disgusting and they were cleaner and more presentable due to them working next to the white slave master's family and inside his home. All around, they were treated with more respect and had access to far more than any African slave who worked outside. However, after a while the fact that these African slaves who were treated far better and taken care of in a humane way became for a better word, "Uppity" towards African slaves who worked outside. Even evolving into the kind of slaves who oversaw the African slaves who worked outside, reporting bad African slave workers and snitching about escape attempts among the African slaves.

The actions of the African slaves who worked inside the white slave master's house and the way they started acting towards African slaves who worked outside reminds me of what is going on in society today. Why do wealthy black entertainers and athletes decide to act so ignorant while white society is watching with a fine-toothed comb to criticize black people? As discussed in detail in a previous chapter, when black people get money and become famous, their actions directly affect the way white society treats black America. While it is the consensus of many people that most wealthy, black and popular individuals do not act appropriately and do not want to be role models in society, our children have little to no chance of acting correctly if they become rich and famous. Once again showing the fall of black people into an even further hole when it comes to being treated better by white society. What does all of this prove, that my dreams are filled with past and historic that have affected the way things are going today.

AFFIRMATIVE ACTION

Affirmative Action was yet again another way for white people to somehow ensure they were on the top of the food chain in business and economic advancement. America got so bad at providing jobs for minority folks who deserved and earned the right to secure a good and high paying job, Affirmative Action needed to be created and publicly diminish even further minorities in America? All the jobs in America were only given to white people and all minorities were out of work? First, I am the kind of person who would only accept a job I know I was going to be treated fairly and with the respect my education and experience demanded. Secondly, the United States government expects me to pay heavy taxes on any income I receive in a calendar year so shutting me out of a job would decrease their revenue a great deal. Lastly, withholding jobs on the National level where such a thing as Affirmative Action had to be created and implemented is just another form of racism falling all the way back to slavery of a people and their advancement in society.

Black people were fine if they worked a remedial and low paying job like sweeping the streets or a janitor, Affirmative Action was not designed for that type of job. It was just when a black person or any minority for that matter decided he or she wanted to e be paid based on their actual education and experience. I remember when Affirmative Action was implemented and I know how upset minorities responded to such an ignorant and literal setup. I guess if I am a minority I need the help of a white person and his stupid pseudo law to have a legitimate chance at being hired for a real and meaningful job. I guess minorities do not want to achieve anything more than a street sweeper status, give me a damn break. The plain and simple fact was business owners did not want to hire minorities over white people until incentive was offered or they had no other choice in the matter. I can only imagine the self-respect of any minority in the business world was already low and falling but Affirmative Action had to be the straw that broke the camel's back.

What is the difference between Affirmative Action and race and gender quotas in college, sports or other major organizations such as the Armed Forces? There is no difference between Affirmative Action and the racial and gender quotas of today. Quotas have always been in almost every organization in the United States for a very long time, even prior to Affirmative Action. How would it look if the PGA, WTA, NFL, NASCAR, NFL, MLB decided to never incorporate black players or include a women's decision? Exactly, the bottom line which governs every business or organization based on earnings would drop like the weather in Alaska or not be as high as it is today. Unfortunately, the media will still cover a black professional athlete's demise in any sport more than a white athlete but we have already covered that topic. When minority people and women started playing and watching a lot more sports the money shot through the roof for these organizations and they have the quota to thank for this prosperity.

According to history and present information, Affirmative Action is still alive and well in the pursuit of leveling the playing ground for minority and women in business, education and politics. I really do not believe this because when an organization wants to be all white or all black or all Hispanic, this is exactly what the organization does in full. It does what it wants and becomes what it wants, even the government only puts minorities in positions based on a quota. Otherwise, President Obama could have made every position in his cabinet black and Hispanic but instead he is hindered to hire a certain amount of minority and women for all cabinet positions. Affirmative Action has the same changing position as racism, never diminishes but changes form while still recognizable. It is all around you and God forbid people of all races open their eyes and see the true effects of what Affirmative Action has accomplished in America.

All that glitters are not gold and Affirmative Action absolutely cannot be defined as Gold or helpful or uplifting in any way possible. I am sure white people and the left-wing politicians who thought they were saving the masses believe Affirmative Action was a positive thing. America probably still thinks it was a positive thing but in this is just another check on minorities and women and a stronger foot on our chest. I know you have heard the sentiment of keeping the black man down, this is exactly what Affirmative Action and quotas have continued to do for a long time. I would rather continue to fight for our rights and equality, something we started hundreds of years ago and continue to this day. Jobs should be earned and given based on qualifications and experience not the color of your skin or the gender of the individual. When will America decide to get this right, who knows!

EVERY DAY IS FILLED WITH RACISM

Can anybody tell me the last time during a complete day something racist was not said out loud, to you directly or indirectly? Also, when this event happened which is usually daily, what did you do about it? Without a doubt and twice on Sundays, racism in some cases is transparent and subtle. As discussed in a previous Chapter, racism can be seen in television shows, commercials and animated cartoons like it is not a crime or big deal in the eyes of black people and other minorities. News flash, it is a very big deal to see racism in any form, especially on television. Have you ever heard a white person compliment a black man or woman by saying, "They look good or are sexy for a black man or woman?" I have heard this when I was younger and recently but when I was younger, I did not realize what was being attempted, presently I destroyed the person with words. Look on television, go into the Post Office, Supermarket, Restaurant, Mall and you will hear racism in its full glory. But be expected to not comment or say anything about it. I am sorry but this black man will never agree to remain quiet when racism is tossed around like a hacky sack on the beach.

The last time I remembered, black people are not the only people who work at McDonalds, Kentucky Fried Chicken, Burger King, Popeye's, Subway and various other fast food establishments. I cannot count on two hands, how many times I have seen the main character in television commercials for these and other fast food establishments and they be black. I go out of my mind when I see this for as many reasons as you can count in your little and racist minds. First, having a black man or woman portrayed like they are happy and enjoy working at a fast food spot is like trying to say this is the only job he or she can do. It is amazing how happy the person looks while talking about a fast food establishment and I hope I see you come in so I can say hello to you with my cheese winning smile. This is so racist and degrading I have turned the channel and thought to myself, why are black people making these commercials and why are the establishments allowing mostly black people to do these commercials. I guess this is the only place black people and minorities can eat. I know this is our own doing because nobody put a gun to their heads and forced them to shoot these commercials but how does it go unnoticed while other topics are in the lime light? The reason is this type of racism is so subtle to the public eye, nobody cares or is even paying attention.

Before President Obama won the office the President, I was watching the presidential election results two terms prior to President Obama winning the office and I could not believe what one of the media coverages said about a black candidate who won some electorate votes. The anchor of a specific network explained, "For the brave candidate, who actually won some electoral votes, we wonder why you even ran for this office?" It was on National television and I do not remember anybody saying anything negative about this publicly racist comment. I do not even want to go into the racism being publicly displayed since President Barrack Obama took office but it is bad and shows how far America has not come on racism. The problem for me comes from the fact people do not even care about racism because it is so rampant in American society it is hardly noticed by even black people.

How racist can you be when most every commercial depicting a normal home owner is white and special loan programs to own homes depict blacks? I just want to comment on this because I know what television is doing when they so cowardly continue to ensure America sees this on television. Television wants you to think the only people who can maintain and own their own homes are white people. How racist can you get and how untrue is this statement? Plenty of minorities own their own homes and have for a long time, the real statistics will never be released because America wants you to think minorities cannot do anything but work at fast food establishments and be on welfare. Wrong answer and completely not true. I would like America to move past the racism and minority status and treat every individual with dignity and respect like it say in the "Constitution."

I was standing in a long line to purchase some groceries from the store and behind me two white people started talking about the shootings of a couple of black people presently in the news. One case involved a traffic stop that turned deadly and the other was a young kid who was walking in the neighborhood with a hood on his head killed by a so neighborhood watch guy who turned out not to be affiliated with anybody but himself. Consequently, these two white guys started saying how they believed the black guys deserved to be shot but not killed because they were causing trouble. The funny thing was I am six-foot, three inches and very muscular about 250 pounds and these two white guys were very skinny and it seemed as if I was not in front of them or invisible. People in front of me and behind them started telling the two men to shut up because I was standing there but everybody is entitled to their own opinions so I told everybody to let the two ignorant men talk. The most shocking thing to me was the callous nature these two men or boys had when it came to speak in a racist way when all reports pointed to negligence of the white people who committed these horrible and unfortunate crimes. This was just an example of how racism is so dulled in the eyes of white people, most will talk about it and show it regardless if black people or minorities are present or not. With, the answer to the original question about racism even being noticed anymore might be, "Not really."

PERCIEVED FOREIGN RACISM

Other countries around the world do not see racism the same way we do in America? I have travelled to several countries all over the world and the reaction to me, a black man almost shocked me in an amazing way. I was not seen as a bad person or a thief or a menace, I was an American and nothing else. They might hate me because I am an American and we beat them in some war way back in history but they do not see the color of my skin. I cannot say this for all countries but most of them I can say were not holding racism in their hearts and loved everybody they encountered normally. I can honestly say foreigners do not find racism until they come to the United States to live but not in all cases. It takes the United States of America to influence and institute racism in a foreign presence.

One country noticeably soaked in beer, was friendly, almost loving and treated every person with the utmost respect in every situation. I retired from the military so travelling to other countries was as often as changing my shirt, but the responses were utterly unexpected. For three years I was treated like a human being in every way possible. The wonderful people in the first Country I visited welcomed me and made me feel as if I should never leave. A great example of this came when I was with me friends and lost in a small city, when we stopped to ask for directions and they realized it was late, the people who were in the cottage brought us in from the cold, fed us, warmed us up and provided a map without asking for a dime or looking at us like we were criminals. The people who were riding with me were black or Spanish and the fact these very hospitable people did not know us from a hole in the wall and treated us so well gave me the impression looks and history were not a factor. Something American society could learn a great deal from and try and master making America a more tolerable option for minorities in general.

Another Country who will remain nameless but has Billions of people, treated strangers with a different kind of hospitality. It almost seemed in this country, the way they treated us was like the United States due to rumors of how black people are normally treated in the USA. I almost felt as if I was being watched very closely every time I went to see the culture of this country with my own eyes. Interesting enough, when I went out with white people, the treatment became almost regale and upper class. I found out the reason why, the country I was in now had the mentality that finding a white American man and marrying him would raise their individual self-worth and status. Marrying a black man was like the kiss of death and very discouraged, insanely I thought this was a joke but found it to be true in this culture. So understandably, we were not considered thieves or thugs but still deemed "undesirably" in this country. I really think it was nothing more than a class level thing and our past- history of slavery puts black people in a lower class without circumstance.

The last part of the world I am going to mention has been fighting an ongoing war and does not care what color or race I might be, but I am an American. They hate me in every way and want nothing more than to see me impending death. This hateful treatment is the kind of treatment any person of any race could respect because it is not concealed or masked for society. If you hate me, let me know you hate me so I can turn my back on you and feel at ease knowing this person hates everything about me. Do not sugar coat it, do not leave me wondering if you want me to leave the country, act as if you hate me so we can get on with our lives. The country I was not exactly visiting gave me that kind of vibe every day I drew breath from my lungs. America could take a lesson from this country as well due to the fact the true feelings of its people is apparent and in their eyes when they look at you. I could not wait to get out of this country but learned a lot of relevant things I put in use to this very day.

Monumentally, other countries pick and choose how to treat black people and I am sure other minorities but the consensus comes from the historical treatment in America. The countries I visited, whether treating me as an equal, shunning me based of the past and present or just straight up hating me because I am American, respond differently to race than the United States history of mistreatment and neglect. Unfortunately, this is the life chosen for black people a long time ago when we were traded for other products all over the world. Is it right to blame other countries for how they respond or react to minorities?

Absolutely not, blame the United States of America for giving black people a negative mark in history. Thank America for delivering a catastrophic point of view of black people to the rest of the world. Something most people in America want to pass over when the talk of race relations is brought up.

UNIFICATION

With all the racial innuendos and confrontations usually contributed to the United States negative racial climate, there are times of complete unity but only due to tragedy. As soon as the tragedy is over and things are back to normal for the most part, racial tension goes from low to high all over again. Attacks on this great country of ours have bonded the races either during conflict or due to recovery. I have lived through some of these disastrous times but far more examples exist throughout history. As stated before, I retired from the Army and wholeheartedly, I saw times when race, creed, religion or gender did not matter even a little bit. We had to come together or not return to our families waiting for us at home. Regardless of the reason or tragedy at home or abroad, these are the times unification and being a human being counted much more than the color of your skin.

Not really the best topic of discussion would be the Civil War which pitted brother against brother and slave or freeman against one another. **American Civil War, also called War Between the States, four-year war (1861–65) between the United States and 11 Southern states that seceded from the Union and formed the Confederate States of America. (Encyclopedia Britannica)** A war based on the right and freedoms of human beings and the economy of the Southern states, a war that should have never been fought because human beings should have never been put into slavery. Anyway, the North and the South fought this war most slaves or black people were given the option to be free or fight for the North. After enlisting into the Army, black Soldiers mostly were used as a labor force for the war but after the North decided it was time for Negro Soldiers to participate, black and white Soldiers fought side by side to help and finally defeat the South in a very bloody and life taking affair. This was the first real time black and white Soldiers fought side by side to stand against a common enemy, even though the Southern Soldiers were Americans as well. A most unfortunate fact, yet a tragic time in our history and unification if only momentarily was achieved.

A very low point in American history but a very huge contributor to unification of all races within the United States of America were the attacks on American soil called the 9/11 attacks. **September 11 attacks, also called 9/11 attacks, September 11 attacks: series of airline hijackings and suicide attacks committed by 19 militants associated with the Islamic extremist group al-Qaeda against targets in the United States, the deadliest terrorist attacks on American soil in U.S. history. The attacks against New York City and Washington, D.C., caused extensive death and destruction and triggered an enormous U.S. effort to combat terrorism. Some 2,750 people were killed in New York, 184 at the Pentagon, and 40 in Pennsylvania (where one of the hijacked planes crashed after the passengers attempted to retake the plane); all 19 terrorists died. (Encyclopedia Britannica)**

This atrocity and futile attempt to inflict death and chaos in the United States prompted unification of every emergency response unit, the National Guard, Firefighters, Police Men, working class and wealthy individuals of every race, creed, religion, color, gender to come together as a Nation and help whoever they could at the World Trade Center Buildings and the Pentagon. People came together and together we came to save the lives of everybody possible. Media coverage showed the tragedy again on television but it also showed people doing what they could as a unified force on the ground clearing rubble and pulling out as many survivors as they possibly could. America even mourned the loss of so many people that day together all over the country and built memorials all over the country commemorating this horrible event in American history.

Another horrific tragedy uniting most people to help one another regardless of race was the hurricane Katrina. **Hurricane Katrina, tropical cyclone that struck the southeastern United States in late August 2005. The hurricane and its aftermath claimed more than 1,800 lives, and it ranked as the costliest natural disaster in U.S. history. (Encyclopedia Britannica)** Although some events associated with hurricane Katrina were not race relation unifying, most of the recovery missions and participation in helping families and individuals out of homes and jobs was universal. I lived in Little Rock, Arkansas at the time and remember how a lot of people were opening their homes for basically refugee status families who had nowhere to stay and who had lost everything. There was no race associated with it, there was no certain people could only stay in certain homes, it was the universal outpouring of help to all who needed it.

Other tragedies in American history have also unified the people of the United States but it is basically ashamed and utterly ridiculous it takes atrocity to bring unity. I wonder if the United States would unify with the entire world if we had to fight against some sort of entity from space. Not saying this is a possibility of happening but I wonder if we could unify long enough to fight against such an entity. If most countries including America cannot even unify within their own borders, how can we come together as an entire world. I just do not understand why it takes so much to achieve something human nature should dictate for us, unification and tolerance of each other. Contrary to popular belief, I do not hate anybody who does not hate me. I would rather be one Nation of unified races and work together as a unit, not fight and see race relations decline as the years pass.

UNWARRANTED AUTHORITY

I am not going to begin to sugarcoat what is going on with Police Officers and minorities in the United States of America at this present time but it is not a positive relationship. Can it get any worse, can trust drop any lower between minorities and the Police? It is getting to the point where almost daily, you can look at your local news channel and see something that has gone terribly wrong with a minority and the Police and hardly any punishment comes to the Police. By the way, did I mention all the Police men I am talking about doing these terrible things are all white! As we all know this has probable been going on for a long time and for many years, such as the Rodney King beating and several unsanctioned shootings of unarmed black men. Unfortunately, the number of incidents among white police officers and black men and women have seemed too increased exponentially. Can this be attributed to anger and frustration or a few bad apples trying to spoil the bunch? I am almost positive; all white Police men do not act in such a manner as to basically commit crimes against the people they are supposed to be protecting.

We have all heard of racial profiling against all minorities, particularly black people and how unfortunate crimes from black people seem to be the highest percentage per capita. More minorities are being systematically pulled over and hassled by the Police creating an increasing opportunity for something to go horrible wrong. Whether it is the minority responding unprofessionally or aggressively to being pulled over which in turn sparks and equally unprofessional and aggressive response from the minority, the outcome is always the same. A majorly bad outcome can include Police brutality, illegal searches, and abnormal behavior such as pulling the individual out the vehicle and a great number of events leading up to an unwarranted arrest in some cases. I have been pulled over while in a vehicle with unruly white men and women and the result is completely different. The Police Officer never raises his voice, threatens to pull the people out of the vehicle and does not stay in his car checking the United States data base for existing warrants. The times I have been present, a verbal warning was issued for reckless driving and obvious intoxication and I could not believe my eyes. One of the times, I was even asked for my credentials and I refused because I was not going to be the next victim of a shooting or a wrongful action.

It is easy to increase the percentage of black people being pulled over and cited for various violations when the percentage of black people being pulled over and harassed are greater. Did you know the average time for a pullover of a minority is almost twice if of most white people? Did you know white people call the police 10 times as much as black people for the same reasons regardless if a crime is being committed or not. The latest example of this happened in Texas at a public swimming pool where white people in the community felt there were too many black kids swimming in the neighborhood swimming pool. The black kids who were swimming had passes and had swam there plenty of times previously to this eventful day.   On National television due to people who videotaped the event after the Police arrived showed a white Police Officer screaming and mishandling young black kids who were merely trying to leave due to the mistrust of white Police Officers. The video tape showed the white Police Officer physically assaulting a young black girl and it was presented on every News channel all week long, sparking several race relation questions. The main question raised during the many discussions on several channels besides FOX news included why did the Police Officer feel it necessary to treat a young black girl so harshly?

I wanted to find the person who called the Police and what exactly did they say to the Police to have them respond to a swimming pool full of black and white kids? Obviously, the person who called the Police was white and mentioned the fact black kids were present. If the same call came to the Police and did not mention black kids, do you really think the Police would have done anything more than a courtesy drive by? You wonder why there is no trust between minorities and the Police, unfortunately due to negative events such as the one in Texas stimulates the hatred and mistrust to a boiling point. What is interesting about this event is why was all the attention put on the wrong issues, such as the black kid's behavior and not the white Police man who was caught on video committing a crime. I am going to let you know something America, if that had been one of my daughters being mistreated like that, I would have found the Police man and treated him the same way in front of his fellow Police Officers. Also, it was never really finalized on what happen to the Police man who did these terrible things on National Television. I can imagine the entire incident was swept under the rug and the Police Officer got away with a slap on the wrist but being on National Television, I am sure the Police department had to respond appropriately in the public eye.

Shooting a person in a stopped car for no real apparent reason during a routine traffic stop is one of the worst incidents I can recall regarding Police brutality or injustice. Not too long ago, this was exactly what happened and the Police Officer was white and the stopped individual was black. Can you imagine the investigation and the scars put in the Police departments all over the country? When do you say enough is enough? When do we stop blaming the entire police department and saying this might be the result of a few bad apples or racist individuals? I cannot truly blame every Police Officer and think they absolutely believe minorities should be treated negatively, shot, beaten, profiled or thrown in jail. Does the shooting of any person while in a parked car during a routine traffic stop seem normal to anybody? This is what I think, racist individuals are sneaking through the Police ranks and waiting for the right time to show their racist side without thinking about the consequences. While they are being ignorant and showing their true side, they are igniting and destroying what little trust minorities have for the Police.   There will be no peace between minorities

and Police until race relations get better in our self-destructing and racist society.

HIDING

How many yahoo post talks about an incident or a minority situation and the comments do not include racism by anonymous and cowardly people? It has gotten so bad, strictly as a convenience if enough people check the thumbs down option, the comment will be hidden due to being a poor comment. Why is yahoo not doing anything about erasing all content deemed racist and vulgar? Anybody can read the comments left on Yahoo and other forms of media as well to include, Facebook, Hotmail, Twitter, Instagram, etc. Is it a positive thing for racist and vulgar comments to be left on a site for all too read, and add their own twist of racism?   It is interesting because the same racist individuals who are leaving these racist and vulgar comments are considered "Cyber Racist" who are virtually in the closet again hiding behind a profile name. I see this as a pathetic form of racism with no face and all the ignorant people who do this need to take a hard look in the mirror. What drives these losers to make racist comments under the cloak of a pathetic profile?

When a black tennis player began to get headlines about a certain look or way they conducted themselves on the tennis court, the amount of ignorant and racist comments started flying around like the wind over the ocean. Comments so negative and ignorant, they are not worth repeating, they brought up another post concerning the racist comments people make on Yahoo on a different site altogether. These "Cyber Racist" wrote words that should have got them thrown in jail and punished severely. With the right and freedom of speech amendment in the Constitution, it is so easy for anybody to say anything if it does not insight a riot or negative protest. In my eyes, when derogatory comments are left about a minority tennis player who has continued to win tournaments as one of the only United States player doing so, I would think the comments would be positive and supportive. I cannot remember who won the Olympics in Tennis, oh yes, it was the same player who people continue to talk negatively about. This same player is the only United States tennis player who steadily wins Grand slams in other countries representing the United States. How about we show her a little respect instead of being the cowards you choose to be hidden behind a screen name on Yahoo. Because when they win tournaments in other countries, they are representing all of us and that alone should garnish your respect and admiration. If she was not a minority, we would not even be having this conversation in a country built on racism, fought for pure racism and hatred, and remains to still be racist at every turn.

Reality television has produced a great number of so called celebrities who in some cases have been in the spotlight for dating minorities and being in the public eye. One in particular, who is the biggest Reality star on this earth has dated minorities as well as the rest of her family. Of course, daily a new situation or activity is publicized about them and the racist comments have never stopped. The most popular racist comments always include why she is dating minorities at all and she is a minority lover and every other useless comment known to man. I did not know we did not have a preference of who we want to date and who we want to marry. Sorry racist, this is not the early 1900s or late 1800s where unfortunately, your racist views were heard and acted upon. Everybody has the ability and right to be with whomever the hell they want to be with and there is nothing your sorry racist asses can do about it. This reality star has made a name for herself, built an empire and her as well as her family has dominated every media outlet possible. Interesting enough, when the tables are turned and a white person is dating a black person who is respected, no negative and racist comments are arbitrarily posted.

Even when the topic posted on Yahoo is one of wrongful or crimes committed against minority people, racism still dominates the comment area. One news story posted on yahoo came from the shooting of a young black boy who was walking home through his neighborhood by a self-proclaimed neighborhood watch man. In the end, this individual was proclaimed innocent due to the controversial "Stand your Ground" Law. "Cyber Racist" of all kinds wrote comments expressing the death of the minority boy was just and warranted without any investigation coming forward. Of course, we all know the outcome of the jury verdict which rocked American race relations but making comments about a young life was deplorable and despicable. If I could look up every individual who made a racist and horrible comment, I would reveal their profile and name so people could see exactly who is making these ignorant comments. That way, the comments would stop because these "Cyber Racist" want to stay hidden like the literal and virtual cowards they represent. No precious life is worth dying regardless of the situation, all matters can be figured out through the laws of the Nation. Nobody has the right to comment on issues concerning life which we all know is not ours to take away or give.

"Cyber Racist" will always be the cowardly, pathetic and in the closet kind of ignorant people we expect them if the media continues to explore every possible way of publicizing in detail racial tension in America. While you are reading this book, please turn on your computers or whatever and look at the news lines of Yahoo, Google, Hotmail, etc. and see if you cannot find at least five major issues or events concerning race relations and racist comments to follow. I promise you they are there and will always be there for the long run. The media emphasizes celebrity, tragedy, government and professional athletics which sell the most especially if race relations are connected in any way. It takes 10 bad stories to find one good story in the news and controversy sells my friend. Can I suggest to all the "Cyber Racist" to spend your time reading articles and publications emphasizing the upward progress of your mind and the clarity of peace between all races and cultures all over the world before it is too late.

TREAT US WITH RESPECT AND EQUALITY

When I walk into a store, library, airport, government building or any place deemed open to the public, see me as a wonderful person, kind human being and an American! Do not see me as a tall black person who is there to cause trouble, steal anything and prejudge me only due to my skin color. Is this so hard in a Nation calling itself the "Land of the Free and the Home of the Brave"? How about people become brave enough to treat me as the kind of person who can contribute to society in a positive way and do not make me act hostile towards you before a word comes out of your mouth. I do not want to be the kind of derogatory person who prejudges you and acts in such a manner to show the wrong side of my true character. Can I count on your support in this manner or do I have to go on living in a racist Country tip toeing around every racist thought acting like I did not hear what I just heard? Do you really think it is going to continue to be acceptable for you to be a racist without any retaliation from any or all minorities?

Who decided to subtitle the word American and felt it rational for white people to only be referred to as American? I am an American, not an African American and it does not stop there because racist white people have indicated through this naming scheme the only true Americans are white. Funny, but the so called Native Americans were here long before white people arrived should be the only ones who should have been called Americans without the subtitle.

Black people through revolting slavery built the economy through blood, sweat, agonizing mistreatment and death. Why are black people not just called Americans when they were here in the beginning and considered part of the original group? Americans encompass us all, every person who is of course legally an American is an American without the subtitle. Military Soldiers, Airmen, Marines, Seaman and Coast Guard are not called out by their races so why should Americans be any different. Understanding in the beginning, the military did separate its' people by race by adding certain names in front of the kind of Soldier Mostly Army of course but this stopped long ago. All Americans are simply American regardless of race.

A wonderful black gentleman helped me and my wife push our car out of the street came from the mouth of a white man one day when I was in the store waiting in line to pay for my groceries. People in the line did not say anything because society is racist down to the core. If the person who had helped them was white, they would have said this wonderful man helped us push our car out of the street. Does anybody see anything wrong with these two statements? Was it necessary for the story to include a black person helped them push their car out of the street? I think America has become so racist and obligatory to the racism describing who helped you is always seen with racial epitomes. Meaning if the person who helped you was not white, racial affiliation will have to be included and described in full detail. The media does the same thing when describing anything negative such as a murder victim or murder suspect. Unfortunately, I do not see this ever changing until this entire generations dies out and our children go their own way, fortunately this generation seems to love celebrities a great deal focusing on their every movement.

Focusing on what I hear is easy in a Nation focused on racism for the most part and unfortunately, I heard from a white person the other day how she would rather wait for a white Police Officer before she received help from a minority Police Officer. Of course, I was standing ear shot and could not believe what I was hearing. Did minority Police Officers go to a different training regimen than white Police Officers? The words coming from this white lady's mouth were amazing and I did think I was standing in white power rally or something. It was just amazing how this came from her lips so easily and convincingly. I truly thought she would ask a minority Police Officer to leave and wait for a white one. What would she do if she was pulled over on the highway in the middle of nowhere for speeding and had such an ignorant request, what do you think the Police Officer would do? Personally, I would give her as many tickets as I could for being a racist individual when my job was designed to preserve and protect the masses regardless of race. People see color too much as an actual deterrent to justice and peace. There are only bad individuals, you cannot decide an entire race is bad because of one bad apple, if this was the case, the entire white race would have to be considered evil, violent, ignorant, racist and simply unworthy of survival. Any questions?

When did any person who is white become the original man in America and warrant the exclusive title of American without a subtitle or precursor? Who decided on African, Muslim, Mexican, Japanese, Chinese, British and a host of other cultures would come before the word American and the answer is white people. As stated earlier in this chapter, white people were not the first second or even third people to come to America and if we listen to historical markers and new developments, Indians might not have been the first people in America either. Regardless of any new outcomes and studies, white English settlers were not the first people in America and have no right to call themselves Americans and all other people who happen to be minorities something else! I fight in the same wars as your, die the same as you, bleed the same as you and live in this great but equally racist country the same as you. I want, I mean I request without caring about your response to be considered American and only American. You might as well call people Men Americans and Women Americans, see how stupid and ignorant that sounds. We are all just people, born and raised in a country that needs to let go of its' racist views and unify based on life and love only. Like I mentioned in an earlier chapter, one day we are all going to need to unify and fight together for a central purpose.

AMERICA'S ACTIONS HAVE PRODUCED RACISM IN EVERYBODY

I do not want you to take this wrong way but everybody is absolutely a little racist due to family upbringing, society, human nature or history. If you are a white woman walking down the street and saw a minority man walking towards you and it was just you two, tell me you did not reach in your purse and grab your phone all while squeezing your purse just a little tighter? You can lie or act unknowingly but I am sure you can think of a time this happened in your lifetime. A group of white men were standing together in a park and a minority man walked by, you cannot tell me the minority man would not tense up and either walk faster or turn around completely. Also, the group of white men probably would think of beating up the minority man because they could get away with it, the minority man's word against all of theirs. Minority professors teach several hundred students at a major university and students avoid the class due to the minority professor, claiming he must not know what he is talking about only because of the color of his skin. Minority doctors either men or women who come into the emergency room and save lives daily scrutinized by white patients who request a white Doctor. A white sprint coach, black swim coach, female football coach, muscular woman, white African studies professor, etc. all great examples of when every individual shows a little racism because once again, everybody has a little racism in their hearts.

What was the first thing people were saying when the possibility of a black President of the United States came to the forefront and was a serious option? Many people were saying this cannot be due to the fact every President of the United States have been white from the beginning, during and after slavery was abolished. It did not matter if this prospective black candidate had an Ivy League education, worked as a Senator and was fully qualified for the job, the fact he was a black man undershot the ability for him to become the President of the United States. On the other hand, how many black people voted for him based on the fact he was black before they knew his qualifications? I assure you, plenty of black people had no intention on voting for any other person in the race after this prominent black candidate represented a strong following based off skin color first and substance second. I am not saying after his election, he was not the most qualified candidate because he absolutely was the best and most qualified but his arrival split the Country down the center and most of that was based on racism. During the election, states damn near wanted to succeed form the Union because a black President was a possibility. Certain areas of states who had never been a prominent force in any election prior to this one came out in force to either vote for this black candidate or strongly against him. It was very easy to see the United States still has a major problem with racism and exactly where the strongest racism still exists. You know exactly who you are and almost exactly where people thought it still existed so strongly.

Our families greatly influence your character and good or bad judgment when it comes to race relations profoundly. When you see a young child illustrating a racist attitude and even using derogatory slang directed at minorities, it is a strong possibility these derogatory views are the same views of their parents. This goes both ways, how many of you have heard your parents talk about not bringing home a date or a significant other not of the same racial persuasion as yourself? Absolutely, this does not point at only white or black people but all races generally. The powerful influence of your family is hard to ignore and is directly imputed into your outlook on life. If your family does not concern itself with race and is open to you finding a person who makes you happy, you will act accordingly and not see color as an issue. The way every person should see the world. Children only want to be accepted properly within their families so this influence is very hard to ignore and most of the time followed without question. Not only is family influence very hard to ignore, the family will usually disown the individual who goes against the grain. Case in point, there are several grandchildren who do not see their grandparents initially based on the parents not accepting the choice of spouses of their children. This choice of course is of somebody who is not the same race as the family. Most people see this as a pathetic attempt to get back at the child but eventually the parents come around and accept their grandchildren. All pointing to the fact how influential and trivial a family can act regarding race and showing how everybody has some racism in their heart.

I am not a psychology graduate but I am sure society will influence the behavior of any individual when it comes to racial epitomes. If a person grows up in a town predominantly white or black and the racial climate tends to be negative towards any other race, this will most likely influence the personality of that individual. Ironically, when this same individual leaves their hometown, they will hang out with groups who act in the same manner as the town they left behind, in other words find people who act similarly to their old friends. This can either be racial tolerance or racial turmoil but either way, the influence from society is strong and mostly racist. When you are with your friends, can you recall any racist jokes or wisecracks directed at minorities and you laughed along with the group? You knew it would not be a good idea to go against the grain or racial tone of your circle of friends and speak up against racial inequality because you wanted to keep your friends. Basically, showing you are either a little racist or a lot and do not even realize it until you are presented with that very difficult choice. Individuals have even committed crimes against minorities due to peer pressure and had no real excuse when caught and told to explain their actions. Unfortunately, racism is deep inside of every individual enough to be bumped to the forefront of your thought processes with a little persuasion and little effort.

Is it human nature to bond with your own kind or is human nature to love all human beings without seeing the color of their skin? Accordingly, this society and what I have seen throughout my lifetime, human nature points directly toward bonding with your own kind for the most part. I have seen people or different races connect as true friends for a good number of years but when the shit hit the fan, drop their friendship and side with their own kind against their true friend. It is human nature to show ones' true colors when the going gets tough or self-preservation presents itself emphatically. It is a hard thing to watch especially when siding with your own kind destroys a good friendship and gets somebody in trouble uselessly and based on a lie. We are all the same on the inside so why must color destroy human nature? I believe human nature has been tainted by a good number of events throughout history and recovery will not be an option if we do not do something as soon as possible to change the outlook on race relations. Are we born with a special hate innate in our hearts and souls towards one another, or do is hate a learning process human kind have mastered perfectly?

The largest and most profound factor of the racism that remains in all of our hearts comes from our past historical events. The institution of slavery alone has permanently focused racism and hate in the minds of all races throughout the entire world but more predominantly in the United States of America. Indians or Native Americans were forced off the land they had occupied for many years by the white man and murdered in millions after being tricked and nearly whipped out of existence. Do you think the Native Americans will ever forgive the white man for doing this or hold hatred in his heart in the form of racism? Same can be said for white people who think they are better than the Native Americans because they accomplished this horrible feat. White men were given Africans who later turned into African Americans or black people who became slaves for over 400 years and suffered atrocities unheard of today. Do you think black people will ever forgive white people for taking the credit for bringing black people to America as slaves and trust anything they ever do? Also, do you think white people will ever look at us as equals regardless of any documentation created or proclamations delivered thusly? Spanish people were forced off land they occupied in a war and moved to another part of the world by white people to complete the United States of America by stealing more land. Do you think they will ever get over this fact and trust white people? I can go on and on about horrific events between races cementing the way we act towards one another to this very day. These events shaped the racism I was talking about present in all people. It does not matter what might trigger deep down racism but it is present in all of us whether you think so or not!

CREATIVITY

Do you honestly think the United States of America developed to its full potential without the explicit creativity, scientific development and extraordinary ideas of other races? If you are one of the many and unfortunate racist individuals who truly believes this country was the direct result of only white productivity and creativity, your intelligence level just went from low too negligent. Unfortunately, throughout American history, the creativity of other races was deemed irrelevant and unrealistic. The result of a lower-class intelligence overwhelming an ironically and incorrectly pegged superior intelligence strangled the creative process in America. Point blank, various ideas and inventions were the direct result of other than white individuals in America and in most instances stolen and shared to the public without proper acknowledgement to the actual creator. Thus, slowing down the creativity and ingenuity of the United States of America in totality.

Racist and incorrectly deemed superior intelligent white people decided early on in American history a black person was far less intelligent than the average white person. Excuse me but was there a relevant testing platform developed specifically to test the intelligence of all people on an equal scale? The unfortunately answer is "Negative" and accordingly the racist white people who decided to enslave an entire race of people and basically wipe out their culture, religion and self-worth in some instances deemed intelligence was based on the color of the skin. I never knew this kind of testing existed and was relevant in any case or circumstance. Pure hate and evil energy was the basis for every decision made during the time of slavery and ensured only racist white individuals were the only people with any influence in America. Almost seemingly destroying any creativity or development of crucial ideas passed from one generation to the next of black people in America.

Without going into detail, progress is accomplished on a collaborative scale and with the help of all people in the United States of America, I truly believe the development of America would have been much faster and stronger. The Black culture has always been a culture of strength and actual intelligence only to progress the entire world forward. If White America was so strong and intelligent why did they decide to enslave Africans, annihilate and move the native Americans to Sovereign land and find a way to not participate in the work that made this Country of ours develop fully. All good questions with a simple answer, laziness and the European way of life which includes having servants and lesser people in their eyes do all the work and take credit for the actions. The true progress and development of the United States of America started far after slavery was abolished and other cultures then provided and shared their creative juices to a Nation of so called unity and togetherness. I think the word America used and still uses is "Melting Pot".

It has been said, the Teacher will always be out done by the Student on every level and the same holds true for racist white people and other races. Of course, I am not saying racist and ignorant white people taught other races anything positive but out doing white people has been accomplished time and time again. I want to put this into perspective when it comes to development and accomplishment. I am saying inventions and advancement have come from other races far more than white people; furthermore, development of the world has progressed due to only other races. Without going into detail and embarrassing all the racist white people reading this book, I will simply say this world stems from the achievements and advancements of all other races. Destroying records and hiding the truth came from racist and Eurocentric white people to ensure all the credit was given to only whites throughout the world. Consequently, with every historical record undug and discovered throughout the world, it is seemingly clear white people have made a habit of trying to inherit the Earth falsely and dishonestly. You could say I am biased in my beliefs but facts are facts and I will let you read actual history and discovery and come to your own conclusions. Holding down another race due to your Eurocentric ways tremendously slowed down the progress and advancement of the United States of America.

Every American invention was developed through the blood, sweat and sometimes deaths of other races. I know you have heard about inventions stolen from individual's due to the lack of knowledge or money necessary to advertise the invention and paten the product. When it came to America, many black individuals were killed or sent away with the threat of death based on inventions and ideas that could have progressed the United States of America drastically. It was like inventors of today who work for specific organizations who create a great product but due to direct use and employment of materials from this organization, the credit goes to the organization and not the individual. Unfortunately, earlier in American history, this was the standard practice of the creative process and benefits to mankind in some cases was the result of these actions. In the eyes of the European machine, newly separated from Europe and now the Americas, other races creating better ways for people to live would have been a serious embarrassment and unrealistic due to the so called white individuals falsely superior intelligence. As I have stated earlier in my encouraging and acknowledging words in this book, I wonder who was the racist, despicable, vile, disgusting and immoral white individual who thought it was a good idea to enslave a race of people and use them as you would use a dog and treat them worse. I find it humorous with all the records in the history books kept by white individuals this fact would be left out completely. What should the black individual do with all the knowledge provided in this book and should we forgive the forefathers and continue making the United States of America a stronger Nation or prepare for a war of the races?

CAN WE UNIFY AMERICA

Can anything be done to persuade the United States of America to unite as one Nation and forget the past while making this Country a stronger and more productively unified Nation? With the turbulent beginnings of the United States of America and present state of mind in our society, it is more than unlikely any kind of unification can be accomplished without a massive and destructive revolution. The consensus of White America is simply based on the fact all other races are unequal to their own. We all know this is not based or grounded on facts but it does point to the horrific and violent tendency of a race of people who strike first and back up their actions with religion and expansion views. I have cited most of these views and essentially excuses used throughout our short history by early and present White America. I personally do not agree any kind of unification can be achieved nor do I believe America will ever be more than a divided and deeply rooted racial disturbance throughout this country.

Regardless of any kind of attempt to unify this country, effective measures have come from facing adversity together as a Nation but unfortunately not lasting through the night figuratively. World Wars and the eternal war on global terrorism have been major issues in the United States and ultimately a unifying force In America. During what other times in history have all races banded together in and out of the military forces and unified as one to fight and defeat our enemies domestically and abroad? Only during these times, racial divides and negative attitudes in our society disappear and become something swept under the rug only for a short time. This is the blueprint necessary for any kind of unification to be possible in this Country. Will it happen, probably not but we know unification is possible but not in the way necessary to make positive and permanent moves in the United States of America.

Why does White America believe they are superior to all other races and continue to control the social climate and racial segregation of America? The answer is the same reason early white slave owners did not want slaves to learn how to read and educate themselves properly or at all. We call this self-awareness and if it happens in America, white domination and power will change dramatically and they will lose their power base completely. Regardless if you believe this to be true, it is the truth and as soon as other races decide to unify first, the chances of the country coming together will never happen. Just because a society started out degrading and virtually destroying all other races besides their own, does not mean it should remain the same old song and dance forever! Other Nations have got this right by starting out caring and giving everybody the chance to achieve greatness, while other Nations have done worse than America in this situation. What happens when you back a dog into a corner? Eventually the dog will have no choice but to attack what is in front of it! Remember this in the next coming years and be ready for the adverse reality of racial separation, unity and revolution.

Violence has been the underlying savior of many revolutions and control used throughout history. It has been said, when a people wanted to conquer another people or lessor people, they resorted to extreme violence and murder. What do you think started the United States of America, revolts against an oppressor who wanted more than they deserved later turning into the oppressed becoming the oppressor and enslaver of another people? What else is there to fear or to lose in the United States of America for all other races? Exactly, nothing is left to lose and we have been backed into an extremely small corner and the resolution is clear and present danger. Consequently, the choice will be left up to American society and development but the only choice I see soon is the same hate once shown to our people will be reversed and directed towards White America.

Just imagine how strong the United States of America could be if the chains of hate and racial equality were dropped into oblivion with the souls of the perpetrators who started it? A huge majority of people in the United States truly believe there is nothing wrong with how this country is portrayed and the state of things. I understand some people do live under a rock and never get out of the house, watch television or read the news but the racial tension in our society is boiling the melting pot over the sides. Do you think people could wake up one day and realize we are all on the same team and have made the United States a wonderful and free place to live? With the minds of every race and important ideas not being washed away or put aside due to pure ignorance, our country could be even better than it presently has ever been. Unification is the key,

unification is the probable outcome and unification will eventually happen

throughout the world regardless of any evil, selfish, destructive or murderous

race.

A NEGATIVELY FORCED BLACK ATTITUDE

The only physical and mental reaction to generations of inequality and degradation is negativity! Strong, educated and peaceful black leaders have tried for many years to find a way to make peace in America but have failed miserably. Within our own government, unpopular legislation is met with resistance and push back from congressional officials. This action is done immediately and with little to no effect on the individuals who are responsible for the legislative friction. Why have black people decided not to push back in such a way the world takes notice? Not one time in American history have black people decisively caused destruction and chaos to make a point. White history only provides examples of death and destruction to either acquire possession or eradicate a people altogether for domination. Black American history needs to add a new section involving an out and out race war. There is no other way to make the kind of emphatic statement needed to ponder the correct response for racism. Racism was made up to destroy the identity of people by attempting to destroy their spirit and self-worth. The Black Spirit is over flowing and about to strike a decisive blow on White America in a dynamic way.

It seems in America the number of racist acts against non-whites are increasing and being swept under the rug and justified not a crime. While Black America continues to riot and complain without action that makes sense, others are gearing up for what will be a strategic, violent and out and out uncivil race war. Non-white people are done standing by and allowing the racist side of White America continue carrying the racist view shared by so many white people over one hundred years ago. Regardless if you wanted black people to remain in America after being used in such a manner to have virtually created and maintained America with their vary soul, lives and pain, just wait, our answer to this question will be here shortly. In my view, black people have waited far too long to act decisively. We have waited and ignored our deepest thoughts on racism and allowed the racist side of White America to proceed unchecked with no consequences for their actions. Actions do not come without responses and the time has come for true retaliation but, the force creating the response to racism is already ready and willing to make it happen now. In my opinion, the time is right to strike in force and dominantly on the racist side of White America, however, ninety percent of White America is racist and that is an estimation based on the media and the last few Presidential elections.

Peaceful demonstrations versus violent confrontations or attacks has been the two choices made by Black America for many years. Let us look at the actual results of both decisions. The dominant way Black America responds to any kind of racism is a well thought out, organized and peaceful demonstration with speeches against the outrageous bad judgement. Sometimes this way of dealing with racism makes the media and local news stations and the word might get out and change a few minds on the subject. Slowly but not surely, the message is heard and received by all of America. This can no longer be the way to get our point across, mainly because it never works in our present day and age. Understandably, past marches, boycotts and strong unity changed some things for the better but peace is not the way the racist side of White America responds to racist issues. Their response included, physical violence, intimidation, vulgarity, ignorance, defamation, murder, rape, lynching and every other negative word regarding racism and horrible acts. There has not been one point in history where racism was not in the forefront when it came to White and Black America and simple equality. When Black America becomes violent and it is towards any part of White America, you can bet your bank account, it will be covered by the National media and shown all over the world insuring Black America looks as negative as possible but this also provides a reaction to a racist action. Examples of this are Police brutality and wrongful death of minorities, Stand your Ground Law and wrongful death of minorities, racist organizational marches and rallies and wrongful death of minorities and more and more violence against minorities on a global scale. The only way to be heard is with a decisive reaction to a racist action. This has already been happening and will continue until it explodes into the limelight and America understands and decides to correct racism publicly.

The time for talking about racism has come to an end in America. The time for embracing thy brother and turning the other cheek in America is over. Racism is at an all-time high and only one thing is going to affect change in

America, an eye for an eye attitude. I am invoking my freedom of speech rights by saying, racism needs to be met with swift and utter carnage. The way White America continues to do starting way back in the 1500s and I am sure further back in history. When white people wanted land or riches or other races for slavery, using the Bible and mixing their own evilness resulted in the annihilation of so many cultures, religion, history and people there is no way to accurately track the true death toll inflicted to the world. It is obvious the world would not mind seeing racist white people get a taste of their own medicine and suffer dramatically. Personally, I still want to turn back time and ensure racist white people could experience slavery and suffer at the hands of themselves for over 400 years, but a systematically defining race war and positive change and view on racism in America would suffice. I do not want my children to experience the kind of racism present in America today. At this point I do not care if all races of children play together or America decides to truly treat every race of people with equality and respect, just not invoke racism in a country unified under one American Flag and Nation. Try to love and respect yourself before you think you can love other people you do not know or understand, just love them as a fellow human being!

I still think of my strong beating heart and intelligent brain pondering the outcome of what will end up a destructive move on racism in America. I promote nothing but the eventual outcome and reversal of racism quickly. I want effective consequences for racist actions in America entirely. I am not saying please or asking for permission in any way, however, I want it to be known all racist white people are being put on notice and whether you like it or not, you will be dealt with sooner than you think. It is not good enough to hide in the closet or be on the internet hiding behind a misleading profile, you will be found and dealt with accordingly. I do not hold hate for anything or anybody but I cannot accept a racist, a racist history or a racist country I helped to protect with my mind, body and soul. Who can be blamed for the racism endured by my generation, moreover, is it as simple as extinguishing the old guard of racism to give America a chance and ability to heal itself? Far too many chances have been given to the racist side of White America to make a change and the time for redemption and revenge is upon us. I still cannot believe or understand I live in a country where black people were murdered on public display as if it were the entertainment for the evening and no justice was ever sought for the countless victims. With this kind of erroneous American History, it will be very easy to strike blows on racism. Very easy!

FREE FINAL THOUGHTS ON RACISM

I wrote this book to invoke the feelings and thoughts of almost every black person walking in the United States and White America. I wanted White America to see the struggles from the inside out of how it is being black in a country that feels sorry for us, while at the same time does not want us around. We were used like a wrapper covering a chocolate bar left out in the sun nobody will pick up and consume. I am glad I am the man I am today, not a politician, not a rich athlete, not a musician or rapper, not raised by a silver spoon but a retired Army Non-Commissioned Officer of 24 years who has seen and lived a great deal. What do black people need to do to get the same respect and equality in a country we basically created and forged with our very lives? Do we need to take it upon ourselves to force action on racism besides talking and praying about it? White America, you might have a friend or two who are black but when they think about you properly, their guard is up and thoughts of injustice and inequality are on their minds. Simply stated, black people do not trust white people any more than white people respect black people.

As I watch the daily news, I see more and more racial tension and incidents consuming the United States and I wonder how it is possible to allow such distention. White cops are shooting and mishandling black people for minor types of crimes ending in death or horrible mistreatment due to the cop's fearing for their lives. Most of the victims of Police violence are scrutinized after the incident and if found to possess any criminal record, publicized for society to see it. Even when the victim was not doing anything wrong except being black at the wrong time or in the wrong place. On the other hand, I also watched a white supremacy rally in which the participants were brandishing weapons and using them against protesters with not even as much as a warning from the Police. How can Police Officers feel threatened by a black person without a weapon and feel safe with a white hate mongrel with a weapon? It even went so far as a white man during the rally had his hand on his gun while the Police were talking to him without reaching for their weapons, how can this be? A black person would have been shot 100 times if they had their hand on a weapon or even possessed one. How is this equal treatment and why would Police Officers claim protection for all citizens? Give me a break!

Now, do you understand why one of our black historical leaders proclaimed, "By any means necessary." This very sentiment strikes loud and clear in our society today even though it was uttered over 40 years ago. Violence is necessary in a land advocating hate and using fear as its main weapon throughout its very existence. Our African ancestor's hearts were stronger and needed change to rectify their lives and spirit but now is the time to punish racism with physical and mental brutality. Racism needs to be wiped out like a plague or disease and destroyed for public display the way racist white people killed African slaves for pleasure. Once again, my mind cannot wrap around the fact my country allowed and participated in such horrible actions. But it did! Would

it be wrong to say I want blood for the atrocities of the past, or should I expect

backlash from this racist society for my words? Either way, I do not really care

about what society thinks of my words, I only care society hears my words and

starts to get my strong message. A message of warnings and actions being taken

against racism without saying a word but swinging a large stick and letting

bullets fly.

Why does America still hate me, you do not even know me or live my

challenging life? I have tried to inform a racist White America I am not a treat to

you and I can help keep this Nation strong from within. It seems you would

rather continue treating me like an outsider even though I am your equal and

beyond. I have created multiple inventions and critical processes conducive to

the progress of America while failing to receive any credit or gratitude. I have

re-written your sports record books in every sport you decided to let me join

decades after its creation. I gave you several types of music which still today

dominate all airwaves and have been incorporated into many product

advertisements. You watch my movies and comedians and entertainment while

laughing, crying and being filled with joy. You gather every Sunday and watch

two types of sports, blacks took to another level while still allowing everybody to

play equally. Something you failed to do and if you had your way would create a

league to this day omitting every race but your own. This would make for a boring sport on every level. It is enough you continue to try and keep me down when I keep jumping back up and screaming equality, justice and fair treatment without reminders of the past kicking me in the face. My children will see a lot more equality than I saw in my life regardless of how we need to make it happen.

I refuse to wake up day in and day out wondering what kind of racist mood America might be in and how they are going to treat my family or myself? Look around America, the revolution is already here and it has nothing to do with talking or demonstrating anything less than retaliation. I am not going to describe exactly what retaliation might mean but if you have read and understood anything prior to this paragraph, you already know the answer to that question. It will come strong and hard and ensure my family and other black families feel safe and without anxiety in America. My heart and soul is stretched and revealed in the face of the African slaves who were used as property, forced laborers and entertainment for a racist and destructive white America. The same America wanting me to celebrate their forefathers and historical dates year after year. Everything that screams America was created or discussed in the hopes only white people in America would succeed as the true masters far after slavery was abolished. THE HISTORY OF THE UNITED STATES OF AMERICA CREATED RACISM BUT THE REACTIONS OF BLACK AMERICA WILL END IT!

APPENDIX

WHAT WE SHOULD DO AFTER THE RACE WAR

We should learn to get along, love one another, inspire our great nation, make progress on a social basis and unify to destroy terrorism and global hate. If these words sound familiar, The United States of America once promised the same thing for its people. For all people! As stated previously in this book, I sincerely question the truth of the American document claiming equality for all! Nevertheless, light will fight through the dark and fill the land with hope and opportunity. We have had great black and white leaders who knew this kind of war was going to eventually happen due to the increase in hatred towards one another. It would be easier and less destructive if the generation of hatred would simply pass without passing hatred to the next generation. I wish I could this very thing happened in America but it did not and moreover, a new President increased the bravery and frequency of hate groups in America ten-fold.

Rebuilding national unity is comparable to a five-force hurricane devastating a city and the city having to start from scratch forgetting about the previous cities structure. There is no possible way we are going to forget the past or want to forget the past. Forgetting the past is not going to help America heal but the outright extermination of racism will put us on the right path. Love is the only thing free in this world and when you utilize correctly, the universe will repay you. Is it really that hard to express love and compassion for your fellow man and woman? The United States of America will be challenged once again to come together and be the United States of America. If people are in each state and they are considered united, why has it taken so long to make this country united? Here are the 10 steps needed to unify this country.

1. Wipe out RACISM in all forms concentrating on becoming one voice in unison.

2. Include all people in the pursuit of happiness and the American dream.

3. Change the rule of Freedom of speech without including racist groups which insight violence.

4. Love one another.

5. Continue building America as the greatest country in the world but include EVERYBODY!

6. See racist people for who they really are and punish their vulgar actions.

7. Government representation based on actual race percentages.

8. Catch up to the rest of the world in education by educating EVERYBODY.

9. Help your fellow man and woman.

10. Leave a mark on this earth in a way that helps at least one person to succeed and be a positive influence on society.

Before I die, I would love to see an America my grandchildren and children do not have to worry about racism or political defamation with non-representation of all races. Love is the standard and everybody provides a helping hand in all situations. Judging people is only done in courtrooms and on an equal standing. I do not need to see all races of kids playing with each other but it would be nice to know their parents are not teaching them any negative differences between the races. People learn about each other through speech and not a stereotype or prejudice. By the way, the only thing needing to be great in this country are the people. Love one another, keep each other safe, do not exhibit hate and be the American citizen our country originally expressed in governmental documentation.

www.ingramcontent.com/pod-product-compliance
Lightning Source LLC
Chambersburg PA
CBHW071224240726
48654CB00009B/915